ON JEWISH LEARNING

FRANZ ROSENZWEIG

ON JEWISH LEARNING

edited by **N. N. Glatzer**

Schocken Books/New York

Parts of this book were rendered into English
by William Wolf

Library of Congress Catalog Card No. 65—25411

ISBN 0-8052-0843-7

Manufactured in the United States of America
10   9   8   7   6   5   4   3   2

CONTENTS

INTRODUCTION   9

THREE EPISTLES

   It Is Time: Concerning the Study of Judaism   27
   Towards a Renaissance of Jewish Learning   55
   The Builders: Concerning the Law   72

APPENDICES
   by Martin Buber and Franz Rosenzweig

   Upon Opening the Jüdisches Lehrhaus   95
   More Judaism! Two Letters   103
   Revelation and Law (Martin Buber and
      Franz Rozenzweig)   109
   The Commandments: Divine or Human?   119

NOTES   125

ACKNOWLEDGMENTS

The three treatises contained in this volume appeared originally as individual pamphlets and were later included in Rosenzweig's *Kleinere Schriften* (Schocken, 1937); they appeared also as a separate volume in the Schocken Bücherei (1937).

The material included in the Appendix is based on the volume *Briefe* (Rosenzweig's letters), edited by Edith Rosenzweig (Schocken, 1935). The parts of the book published here in English for the first time have been translated by William Wolf. The remaining sections were taken from *Franz Rosenzweig: His Life and Thought*, presented by Nahum N. Glatzer (Schocken and Farrar, Straus and Young, 1953).

Martin Buber has graciously given his permission to include in the Appendix an English rendition of his letters to Rosenzweig on the theme of *The Builders*. They appeared originally in the Schocken Almanach on the year 5697 (1936).

INTRODUCTION

I

Franz Rosenzweig's essays and articles on Jewish learning are being presented here in the hope that his reflections might be of some relevance to present-day discussions of the subject. It is well realized that Rosenzweig's words were spoken a generation ago and were addressed to Central European or, specifically, German Jewry. Therefore, Rosenzweig's analysis of the situation of Jewish learning cannot be applied *in toto* to the American, British, or South African Jewish community nor can his projects be easily transplanted into another climate. Yet, much can be gained from a study of Rosenzweig's fresh approach to the problems of emancipation and assimilation, from his bold attack on stuffiness and ignorance, from his fervent faith in the possibility of a revitalization of classical Judaism. The problems that concerned him are still with us, however different, and most probably their manifestations will continue to stir the sensitive among us as long as there are Jews in a world of nations, states and civilizations. Rosenzweig, who so profoundly believed in translation as a great cultural instrument in inter-human communication (ultimately there is only *one* language, he said), should be granted the right of being heard in the community of his brethren in other lands and other generations. It may then be discovered that beyond the differences of background, conditions, aspects and opinions we really speak one language after all.

People usually grow weary when they hear an educator extolling the virtues of knowledge. What else should an educator do? It is different, however, when a "nonprofessional" raises his voice. Rosenzweig is the Jewish "layman" of modern times who broke the monopoly of professional teachers and rabbis as "experts" qualified to talk on the study of Judaism. He even ventured to doubt the authority of some official spokesmen of Judaism to speak of issues of which they were no longer informed, and encouraged those troubled about the sorry state of events to speak up on the great issue of which they were not yet informed but which had become a major concern of their lives: living Judaism. Rosenzweig refused to conform to the modernist division of the Jewish community into "experts" and "laymen" and in his own writings and activities he cut right across the lines. He is not only nonprofessional but also strongly unconventional in attacking the central theme of Jewish civilization.

Rosenzweig wrote *It Is Time* (*Zeit ists*) at the Balkan front in March 1917 shortly before he set out to formulate his philosophy. In this epistle on Jewish learning and education, Rosenzweig first analyzes the state of Judaism in Central Europe. He criticizes both Jewish scholarship way to the sources of Jewish life." But Guttmann could speak as he did, without hurting his professional reputation, because the new attitude to learning did not imply a weakening of the scientific spirit or a lesser emphasis on meticulous research. The twentieth century scholar was to add a new responsibility to the ones carried by his nineteenth century colleagues. Guttmann points to the short-comings of the old Science of Judaism: the historic analysis of Judaism had silenced almost completely any attempt to understand its philosophy; even within historic studies archival research had taken precedence over a consideration of tendencies and of meaning; history of literature had remained a collection of biographies of scholars and rarely penetrated into the "intellectual content of literary creations and the underlying ideological and emotional motives." Jewish piety or the structure of Jewish community life never became a theme of study. Problems arising from present-day needs the old Science of Judaism had left to popular enlightenment and apologetic literature to solve. The young generation of scholars will not repeat such shortcomings, Professor Guttmann argued; it will not evade the requirements of the hour. This new attitude, which should be the driving motive of the Academy proposed by Franz Rosenzweig, will bring about a "rejuvenation of our science."

The work of the Academy was pursued in six disciplines: Talmud, Philology, Philosophy, Literature, History, Economics and Statistics. Among the books published by the Academy were studies by Chanoch Albeck about the composition of the Mishnah and about the halakhic midrashim, a critical edition of the Midrash rabba to Genesis (Judah Theodor and Chanoch Albeck);

Fritz (Yitzhak) Baer wrote about the sources and the composition of the *Shevet Yehudah* and started on his monumental *Die Juden im christlichen Spanien;* Selma Stern contributed a book on the Jew Suess and a collection of material, skillfully interpreted, on the Prussian state and the Jews. Leo Strauss issued an important analysis of Spinoza's critique of religion (*Die Religionskritik Spinozas als Grundlage seiner Bibelwissenschaft*); Fritz Bamberger wrote a thoroughgoing discussion of the philosophical system of Maimonides. The Jewish writings of Hermann Cohen were edited by Bruno Strauss and published in three volumes; Rosenzweig wrote the introduction in which he traced Cohen's development from a philosophical academician to a Jewish thinker. The general philosophical and political essays by Hermann Cohen were edited by Albert Goerland and Ernst Cassirer. On the occasion of the two-hundredth anniversary of the birth of Moses Mendelssohn, the Academy initiated a project of publishing the collected works of Mendelssohn in sixteen volumes. Up to 1934 six volumes appeared. The research program of the Academy was headed by Eugen Taeubler who succeeded in inspiring young scholars with the ideal of Jewish research. In 1929 after ten years of activity the Academy published a volume of essays by the spokesmen of the institution, Leo Baeck, Ernst Cassirer, Ismar Elbogen, Isaac Heinemann. Rosenzweig presented an as yet unpublished lecture by Hermann Cohen on Spinoza's relationship to Judaism. Julius Guttmann again viewed the principles of the Academy and pointed to Rosenzweig's original way of relating scholarship to life and of emphasizing living rather than two-dimensional research.

The importance of the work done by the Academy cannot be overestimated. When, in 1934, the Academy had to cease functioning and transferred its stock of published books and the program of some outstanding projects to the Schocken Verlag, it could be looked upon as the crowning chapter in the history of modern Jewish scholarship in Western Europe. And, true, there was a marked difference in outlook between the nineteenth century Wissenschaft and the Academy. But in the final analysis the Academy, too, was not concerned with rejuvenating Jewish life but was primarily interested in the investigation of historical facts. There was no way of tracing the results of scholarship upon the reading or listening audience, no way of communicating the scholar's insight to the learning youth.

Foreseeing this development, Rosenzweig turned his back on the Academy as soon as its sponsors had decided to divorce research from the teaching activity of the scholars he had advocated in *It Is Time* (*Zeit ists*). Perhaps he was asking too much, perhaps he underestimated the force of convention. He confessed that he considered "scholarship (*Wissenschaft*) a means and education the end," adding that "of course the means has to be treated as if it were an end in itself because there is no other way of engaging in scholarship." It was possibly too much for Rosenzweig to expect to find scholars who would accept an "as if" attitude in scholarship which he himself rejected in philosophy. In a letter from Warsaw, where he saw the intimate union of Jewish learning and Jewish life, he wrote: "A mere Academy for the science of Judaism matters as little to me as an academy for the science of Botokudoism." Thus, though Rosenzweig remained connected with the Academy and even contributed to its program, he gave his passionate support to a new plan which he outlined in *Bildung und kein Ende,* here published under the title, *Towards a Renaissance of Jewish Learning.*

In this essay, written early in 1920 and addressed to his friend Eduard Strauss, Rosenzweig laid the foundation of the Freies Juedisches Lehrhaus in Frankfort on the Main. In this pamphlet Rosenzweig criticized the Science of Judaism for having lost confidence in its own cause. Both its schools and its scholarship languish through lack of foundation in Jewish life. The platform of Jewish life, Rosenzweig argued, had been abandoned in the process of emancipation. The need is felt again, however, for a more profound Jewish life. Not new books but a new Jewish man is needed.

The Lehrhaus in Frankfort, which Rosenzweig headed from 1920 until his death, tried to educate this new Jewish man. Rosenzweig believed that a renewal of traditional "learning," a renewed contact with classical Jewish writings could restore something genuinely Jewish to the Western intellectual. Well he realized that the modern Jew stands on the periphery of Jewish life—he had experienced this position in his own past—but he considered possible a movement from the periphery to the core. The old learning had led the Jew from the text to the world without; the new learning will have to lead from "without" to "within." The "return to the sources" thus became the watchword of the Lehrhaus. The public lectures delivered on high sounding topics by famous figures were a means of arousing interest in the whole project, in stimulating the community to talk and the press to write about it and in attracting the more serious students to the small study groups and seminars in which the actual work was done. The main emphasis was on the Hebrew language as the key to the great documents of classical Judaism and on the Bible and its commentaries. Around this core a wide program was arranged in concentric circles. Jewish history was well represented but historicism, so typical of the Science of Judaism, was carefully avoided; instead, a synchronistic attitude prevailed.

Rosenzweig's confidence in the workability of his plan knew no limits. In a pamphlet, written at the suggestion of Martin Goldner, then the executive secretary of the Lehrhaus, Rosenzweig passionately defended the cause of Jewish "learning," the old and the new. In distinction from a lecture or even from a good university seminar, "learning" implies a patient examination of sources and a patient consideration of what a book has to say. Nothing is known in advance. This attitude, however, only the unprofessional man can manage: only he will take the naive questions of the other fellow more seriously than his own clever answers. A mixture of boldness and modesty is required for "a pursuit so dangerous and yet so necessary." For "while this unsupervised learning is indeed dangerous, it is necessary in a time of transition, when the old teachers, the scholars, are no longer recognized as guides, and the new ones have not yet appeared."

The Lehrhaus in Frankfort functioned seven years. After 1926 only occasional lectures and meetings were held. In 1933 the Lehrhaus was reopened under the directorship of Martin Buber and played a decisive role in

preparing the Jews of Germany to react to the events of
the time—as Jews.

I I I

The treatise *The Builders* (*Die Bauleute*), written in
the summer of 1923 and addressed to Martin Buber,
takes the fateful step from Jewish knowledge to Halakhah, the structure and body of the law, and to the *Mitzvot*,
the commandments and their observance. Western Judaism after the Emancipation (outside of authoritarian,
fundamentalist, Orthodoxy) reduced the wide scope of
the Law to "rituals and customs," sancta of the Jewish
people, or just folkways. It ceased to be a problem of
Jewish religion. "Revelation" could take on no new theological or philosophical meaning; the "Law" was no
longer understood as the expressed will of God and
was—theoretically at least—considered obsolete. A law-
free, antinomian attitude, which earlier periods in Judaism arrived at after mighty convulsions in the soul of
the people, was uncritically accepted as a natural development in modern times.

Rosenzweig, the re-discoverer of classical Judaism, had
to give the issue of the Law his close attention.

In the central section of the *Star of Redemption*,
written in 1918, Rosenzweig discusses Revelation and
the commandments. Yet, here, commandment is sharply
distinguished from the law, i.e., the body of precepts,
statutes, regulations, which organize life under God,—
the law so fundamentally important in *The Builders*. In
the *Star of Redemption*, commandment means almost
exclusively one thing: Thou shalt *love* the Lord thy God!

The imperative of love originates in the immediate presence of the loving God and the beloved human soul. It is this concern with "presence" which characterizes the "Thou shalt" as a commandment (*Gebot*); any thought of the future, any provision for a continuation would turn the immediacy of the commandment into "law." All commandments may—as time goes on—turn into laws; the supreme commandment, the imperative of love, may not. The reverse process may set in: future-directed provisions, laws, may be illumined by the light of the commandment and converted into instruments for the fulfillment of the one commandment to love God—today.

The idea of commandment helps Rosenzweig to understand the social implications of "love thy neighbor," the sacred year in its sequence of Sabbaths and holidays, and the most intimate expression of faith, prayer. Rosenzweig's presentation of the inner life of the faithful, deeply moving in its utter simplicity, is a classic of religious writing. But one must needs realize that Rosenzweig's biographical position while he was writing the *Star* did not allow him to see in Judaism, as far as its law structure is concerned, almost anything outside of liturgy and social justice.

Yet, while Rosenzweig was writing the *Star of Redemption* he had been undergoing experiences which led him later to a decisive change of position with regard to Jewish law. He had come in contact with East European Jewry, great parts of which bore the "yoke of the Torah" and studied and fulfilled its laws. The *Star of Redemption* indeed makes mention of the "yoke of the Torah" (III, 198) and quotes the talmudic statement about the "oral" or rabbinic dicta which are considered weightier than "the words of the Torah" (II, 102). But these are passing remarks without consequence in the system of the *Star*. Only after Rosenzweig had completed the *Star*, returned from the war, married and established a home, started to direct the Lehrhaus and joined the Talmud study group of Rabbi Nehemiah A. Nobel, only then did "Law" take on a new importance for him.

The reader does well to keep in mind that Rosenzweig, the theoretician and thinker, was strongly determined by the impressions of his senses. The actual, bodily experience came first; the formula, the theory, the system, followed. Whenever the written word was not directly based on living action, it was clearly the longing for action which prompted Rosenzweig to speak.

It is very probable that the Frankfort experience of Jewish observance—beautiful and moving in spite of its rigidity—and the intimate contact with the conservative Rabbi Nobel confirmed in Rosenzweig the view gained in Warsaw that "it can be done." *The Builders* argued that, just as knowledge can be acquired only by the individual's delving into that knowledge, so practice—which is just as knowledge an integral part of Judaism—can be understood only by practicing. A pragmatic approach indeed.

As in the realm of Jewish "learning," so here, in the realm of law, what is being done must be transformed from mere substance and matter into inner power. In order to make this clear Rosenzweig, resuming the terminology used in the *Star*, distinguishes between the two German terms for commandment. *Gesetz* means to him the cold, objective, neutral paragraph of the code, the substance and matter of the law; this *Gesetz* must be transformed into that which it was when it first issued from its divine source: *Gebot,* the living, unmediated call to action which the divine creator demands of the human creature. Man's response cannot be an unquestioning bearing of the law or slavish obedience to its letter; it can only be a loving acceptance of what his present situation in life—his inner ability—allows him to accept. The personal ability to fulfil the law must decide. We choose; but the choice is made in absolute honesty and in a readiness to increase our responsibilities.

This strictly undogmatic and apparently liberal approach to the problem of Jewish observance should not detract our attention from Rosenzweig's actual purpose: to regain for the law the central place it once occupied in Jewish life and to re-establish the connection between the theological concept of divine revelation and the register of rules for human behavior. These are not "customs and ceremonies" but laws of God. There *is* an intimate relationship between a minute detail of Halakhah and the lofty "I am the Lord thy God."

This was the cardinal point to which Martin Buber, the addressee of *The Builders,* objected. His letters to Rosenzweig which appear here for the first time in English (see Appendix) show beneath the friendship between the two men an abysmal difference of opinion. Had Buber given Rosenzweig a full-scale answer, the exchange of views might have become one of the major religious debates in modern Judaism. Buber, who quite often in his career engaged in heated polemics, did wise to exercise self-restraint in not accepting Rosenzweig's challenge and reacting only in these short letters. Buber denies any *direct* connection between revelation and the tradition of binding legal institutions and rites which regulate Jewish life, private and public. He knows fully well that civilized man is by nature a "receiver of the law"; but God is not a "law giver." In his great *Herut*, a "lecture concerning youth and religion" (1919) which had prompted Rosenzweig to address *The Builders* to Buber, the latter had gone far beyond the determined but friendly criticism of his letters to Rosenzweig. In *Herut* Buber advocated a renascence of original religious forces which would enable man to answer the call of the absolute. Such a revival of religiosity would concern men as a whole and would be of universal relevance. Fixed forms of thought and action are not only not necessary; they are inconsistent with, and contrary to, the freedom of man confronting the divine. In later writings (*I and Thou*, "The Man of Today and the Jewish Bible," and other essays) Buber further explored the meaning of revelation as meeting between God and man. But *Herut*, in spite of the preliminary nature of terminology and definition, stands out by a clear-cut position outside of the Law: meta-nomianism. This position of Buber is significant because it was not preached from an anti-religious viewpoint; it resulted from Buber's affirmation of Jewish faith and religion in general.

It was this stronghold that Rosenzweig attempted to conquer by pointing to the fullness of Jewish life expressed in the Halakhah, to the universal implications of the law in classical Judaism—and by dismissing the ultimate theological problem involved. Rosenzweig needed no theological theory when life itself—lived under the law—testified to the presence of the divine.

All Buber could do was to respect the position of his

friend with whom he taught at the Lehrhaus and with whom he translated the Bible. No agreement was possible between Buber, who in his *I and Thou* became the spokesman of a new, universal, religious and philosophical orientation, and Rosenzweig, who found his peace in the practice of Halakhah where the enthusiasm of divine love is translated into the word of daily prayer, the longing for salvation is resolved in the sober conformation to the Mitzvoth, and the ecstasy of religious experience is silenced by the commanding word at Sinai and the scrupulous interpretations of the Sages.

IV

We had quoted Rosenzweig as having objected to being read and having wanted to act and inspire action. He knew, as every good teacher knows, that a student will not accept everything he is being offered; he will listen and then think for himself. In advocating Jewish learning, Rosenzweig wanted to free the student from a narrowness of vision, from parochialism, from departmentalization and factionalism. Once again Judaism appeared in its ancient profundity and universality of concerns. Rosenzweig points to this vast area and invites us to see for ourselves, and through learning and action to become partners in the life process called Judaism. It would be unjust to read his writings, even its programmatic portions, as dogmatic pronouncements which are to be accepted or rejected. The concluding words of *The Builders* allude to the motive of Rosenzweig's treatises and letters: he wanted to reopen the silenced dialogue between the presently living generation and classical Judaism.

NAHUM N. GLATZER

THREE EPISTLES

IT IS TIME:

Concerning the Study of Judaism

To Hermann Cohen

Dear Sir:

If I am submitting the following thoughts and opinions to you in writing, it is because there is hardly a chance that I shall be able to express them to you orally in the near future. I do not wish to withhold them any longer: life is short, and every moment is valuable. I direct these thoughts to you especially, because the majority of those German Jews who intend to live as Jews in Germany honor you as their intellectual leader. Whether we agree with the intention of these German Jews or whether we do not, it is only on the basis of this assumption that we can recognize the task of our time. A policy—and this is what the following thoughts wish and ought to present—must grow out of the soil of the actual state of affairs.

This actual state of affairs in Germany allows us to narrow down the problem of Jewish education to that of religious schooling. This problem in turn can be restricted to the question of religious education in the various types of secondary schools, since the overwhelming majority of German Jews live in the big cities. The largest and most influential sections of our intelligentsia have received their religious instruction from a few years of "religious classes," and some High Holiday sermons. It has been recognized for some time that it is time for a change, and some attempts at it have already been made. However, the particular problem has not been recognized clearly enough.

The resolutions of the Rabbinical Assembly which dealt with these things in the summer of 1916 make it appear, consciously or unconsciously, as if the main difficulty, aside from organizational ones, were the same with which Christian religious education is confronted: the difficulty of developing religious feeling by influencing the intellect. In reality, however, the problem of Jewish religious instruction is quite different. We are not concerned with creating an emotional center of this world to which the student is introduced by other school subjects, but with his introduction into the "Jewish sphere" which is independent from, and even opposed to, his non-Jewish surroundings. Those Jews with whom we are dealing have abandoned the Jewish character of the home some time during the past three generations, and therefore for them that "Jewish sphere" exists only in the synagogue. Consequently, the task of Jewish religious instruction is to re-create that emotional tie between the institutions of public worship and the individual, that is, the very tie which he has lost.

At first sight, such a task may seem to be dwarfed by the exalted concept of "religious education." But if we consider to what a degree our institutions of public worship have become the sieve as well as the reservoir for whatever had survival value in the three thousand years of our spiritual history, we shall have to admit that within their seemingly narrow sphere everything desirable is included. To talk only of the literary documents: The biblical literature of antiquity may be seen as the source and the foundation of everything that is living in Judaism, its encyclopedic expression may be found in the talmudic and rabbinic writings of later times, its sublimity may be discovered in the works of the philosophers—but all this notwithstanding the prayer book will forever remain the handbook and the sign post of historical Judaism. He to whom the prayer-book is not sealed more than understands the "essence of Judaism"; he possesses it as a portion of his inner life; he possesses a "Jewish world."

This phrase will guide us. He may possess a Jewish world, but he is surrounded by another one, the non-Jewish world. This fact cannot be changed, nor does the majority of those with whom we are here concerned wish to change it: nevertheless, they wish to renew that Jewish world. But "to possess" a world does not mean to possess it within another world which includes its possessor; thus the German may possess another civilization—ancient or modern—because and insofar as it also belongs to the spiritual universe which includes him; therefore he can acquire it without leaving his own world, maybe even without understanding its language; because in any event he will understand it only as translated into the "language" of his world; and experience has always shown that knowledge of the words of a language does not necessarily imply "possession" of its civilization.

With our own problem, things are quite different. It is true that the world to be acquired also belongs, in a very important sense, to the fundamental forces of the surrounding world, but it is not to be acquired in that sense. Our own Jewish world ought not to be experienced as a mere preliminary stage to that other world. Such a procedure may be permissible for others, but not for us. For the Jew, Judaism is more than a power in the past, more than a curiosity in our own era; to us it is the goal of the future. And since it is future, therefore it is a world of its own, quite aside from the world which surrounds us; and since it is a world of its own, therefore, it is rooted in the soul of the individual, with a language of its own. The German, and even the Jew qua German, can and will read the Bible as Luther, Herder or Moses Mendelssohn read it; the Jew can understand it only in Hebrew. And even though in the case of the Bible both possibilities must be admitted, because both Jew and German share in its possession, the language of Jewish prayer is different; of the language of Hebrew prayer we may state quite categorically: it cannot be translated. Therefore the transmission of literary documents will never suffice; the classroom must remain the ante-room leading to the synagogue and of participation in its service. An understanding of public worship and participation in its expression will make possible what is necessary for the continuation of Judaism: a Jewish world.

From these premises I shall now attempt to draw a picture of the form and the procedure of such an instruction. What I have to say may not be final; but only a deliberately one-sided, albeit preliminary, choice among many possibilities can guarantee the distinctness necessary for a common understanding. First, therefore, the general plan; since everything needed for its realization under present circumstances will follow later.

We take only for granted what already exists fairly generally in our schools: two lessons per week, amounting to eighty per year, covering nine years of schooling, from the ninth to the eighteenth year of life. We shall soon have to mention a new demand which the public school authorities will have to fulfill. Since, furthermore, the German school system is not likely to undergo any drastic change in the near future, we assume that, as is now the case, a foreign language is taught in the very first year.[1] We also assume that at that time the student knows only certain parts of "biblical history," which is to say that he has no Jewish knowledge worth mentioning. Therefore the backbone of the instruction will be that domain in which the independence of the Jewish world is best expressed today: the Jewish "sacred year," as fixed by the Jewish calendar.

By being introduced into the Jewish week and into the yearly cycle of Jewish festivals the student can be taught the most important customs and institutions related to them. With this foundation he can be given, with the aid of topics selected from Scripture and legends, a presentation of biblical history. The teacher will have to treat the Sabbath and Holidays in the same manner as he explains the origin and intention of the Passover

Haggadah. He cannot strive after completeness, a lively method is all that counts. To give detailed prescriptions is neither necessary nor hardly possible. By and by, avoiding grammatical explanations as much as one can, brief Hebrew selections should be added to the lessons. It is sufficient, during this first half year, to translate, in the ancient method of rendering word by word, selections such as the *Shema Yisrael,* the first and last benedictions of the *Amidah,*[2] several other benedictions, especially those used at the Friday Evening Services, passages recited while taking the Torah out of the Ark and returning it; and, depending on the season of the year, some paragraphs relating to the holidays, e.g., part of *Maoz Tzur,*[3] The Four Questions, the Decalogue, the Sacrifice of Isaac, *Avinu Malkenu.*[4]

For two reasons the more rational grammatical method should not be used at the outset: first of all, it is advisable not to burden religious instruction with difficulties of acquiring a language; such should rather wait until these have been tackled in the first year of foreign language instruction. Secondly, the traditional method, in spite of the drawbacks of greater intricateness and short-lived results, has an advantage which should not be underestimated: the student is not introduced into a dead grammatical structure, but learns, by its actual use, the Holy Tongue as a living language. Consequently, when the time for teaching grammar does arrive, a certain store of examples is already at hand. For this is just the difference between learning the grammar of one's mother language and that of a foreign tongue, that in the latter the student progresses from the rule to its applications, and in the former from its application to the rule. We may anticipate that, when learning the conjugation of a Hebrew verb, the student will remember some language data which, at their first occurrence, had not been grammatically understood, e.g., to remain within the framework of the passages mentioned above: "Who took you out," "and thou shalt love," "Who hast given to us," "We have sinned," "and worship foreign gods," "and they both went together."

However, during the second term of the first year it might be advisable to offer some grammatical instruction, so that by the end of the first year the most important aspects of the noun, pronoun and regular verb will have been assimilated. Whatever is lacking, especially the irregular verb, should be taught in the first term of the second school year. The time lost during the short period of mechanical translation will easily be recovered by the greater ease with which grammar can be taught, since the student is already familiar with so many examples. Generally speaking, not too many difficulties should be anticipated. As long as exceptions are disregarded and only the skeleton of the most important rules is presented in a systematic manner, the rest will be acquired by practice. By teaching grammar in the manner outlined, it will not be too difficult to press this part of the instruction into about fifteen minutes of the daily lesson: the whole material can thus be taught in seventy or eighty periods, devoting to it one quarter of an hour for two years.

The second school year therefore finds the student in command of a certain knowledge of the Hebrew language which should make it possible for him to study, in selections of course, the first book of the Torah with increasing speed. In addition to this, there will be time remaining for the reading of the essential parts of the daily prayer book, at least those sections recited on weekdays and Sabbaths; those passages which present difficulties of language or content, e.g., some Psalms and the *Sayings of the Fathers*,[5] should be omitted. This material may lead to other subjects. Biblical history will no longer have to be taught as a separate entity, since the child has already become acquainted with the venerable patriarchs in their own language; the great moments of those stories will be engraved upon his mind, not in a pale imitation, but in all their originality. Instead of the lame words, "Where art thou?" from the Paradise story, and "Here I am" from the Sacrifice of Isaac, he will remember the concise and concentrated Hebrew terms. How senseless and unsuitable is it anyhow to send Jewish children into life knowing the primary expressions of their faith only in translation! Language and meaning are co-related, and we underestimate the intimate relation existing, even before Luther, between Christianity and the German language, if we think that Jewish contents can be clothed in German language without admitting connotations foreign to them. This becomes worse if the memory is filled with such material. It is certainly not harder to engrave upon a child's unburdened memory a psalm in its original sounds than in the very dubitable "German" of the current translations. In this distribution of the material of the second year the calendar will have to be neglected. This is necessitated by a more thorough treatment of the patriarchal history and the cycle of the daily and weekly prayers.

In the third year the student, after the two preceding

years of instruction, will already be able to study the Torah more fluently. This should, as much as possible, be done following the sequence of the weekly portions of the Torah. But even now completeness is impossible; only selections can be offered. I cannot state whether the selection should be left to the individual teacher, or a special school edition should be used. During this year, after the daily prayer book has been studied, selections from the holiday prayer book and the Passover Haggadah shall be introduced.

After the preparation outlined above, it is important that the student, having his Bar Mitzvah in sight, be given an opportunity to take part in the Sabbath services. For this, the cooperation of the school authorities is needed.[6] The high school of one city, or, in larger cities, those of one district, should revise their weekly schedule so that one of the two or three weekly periods of instruction in Christian religion will be held on Saturday mornings. This should be done from the third school year through at least the fifth year and, if possible, even longer; but this will depend on the number of teachers giving instruction in Christian religion. Thereby the Jewish students will gain one hour, and, counting the recess periods, even seventy-five minutes[7] during which they can visit the synagogue. The Jewish community should in turn be responsible for two things: services should be held at a place not more than ten minutes' walking distance from all the schools of that district; moreover, they must be conducted in such a manner that the part of the services covered within this hour include the reading of the Torah, that is to say, from the removal of the scroll from the Ark until its return. It would be excellent if this service is at the same time the main service of the congregation; if not, we should remember that a short secondary service will be no less impressive than the official one. It will certainly be more purposeful than an artificial "youth service," which does not fulfill what is the very purpose of such an institution: the introduction into the very life of the congregation. Of course no student should be forced to attend such services. The impetus must come from the classroom and the technical possibilities from the school authorities. Considering the close connection between the instruction and the synagogue, it is self-evident that the Hebrew pronunciation used in the classroom must be the same as that used in the synagogue, only then can the feeling of being-at-home, which is requisite to the consciousness of a peculiar Jewish world, arise.

In the fourth school year the calendar will reappear. The study of the commentary of Rashi will now be added to that of the Torah; of course here, too, only selections can be taught. Rashi, that great and popular commentator, who transmitted to the second millennium of the Exile the vast treasure of the first, will gradually introduce the student into the spiritual world of the Talmud and Midrash—a world which, even in our own times, has had a greater influence on the Jewish character than we know or admit. The teacher must be left responsible for broadening with care and reverence the view of Jewish history, allowing the student some glimpse into those forces of Judaism which were foreign to Rashi and became strong only after him. By this time the student will have had enough experience in reading Hebrew that unpunctuated texts can be introduced in place of punctuated ones. The study of biblical history will be completed by a cursory reading of the more important passages of the narrative books from Joshua through Nehemiah. It should be noted that during this year the average student will enter the congregation as a Bar Mitzvah. The moment of the Bar Mitzvah has unfortunately lost much of its meaning in the last decades. After the preparatory course, as outlined, it will regain its dignity, especially if it is restored to its pristine simplicity and freed from all harassing examinations and tests.

At the end of the next two years a very important group, namely, the future businessmen, leave school;[8] therefore, by this time, Jewish religious instruction must be brought to a somewhat rounded conclusion. In the first of these two years the connection with the yearly cycle of Bible readings is maintained by the study of the prophetic portions, the Haftarot. This study, especially that of some specific sections from the prophets, may lead to a primitive discussion of Judaism vs. Christianity. Also, the *Sayings of the Fathers* may be discussed at this stage; these basic formulations of Jewish Ethics on the one side and, on the other side, selections from the Mishnah and the Codes, especially those dealing with the more important religious practices, will bring the knowledge of practical Judaism to a preliminary conclusion.

The second of these two years will similarly conclude the knowledge of spiritual Judaism. The point of departure shall be the Book of Psalms, e.g., those chapters not yet studied as part of the Prayer Book, and, allowing the teacher to use his own judgment, other chapters from Scripture not yet discussed. Also a short synopsis—not

more—of the development of Jewish thought in connection with the general fate of the people should be given.
Finally, it seems to me that the student should not be
dismissed without having had a glimpse at the most
peculiar and, in many respects, the most important pro-
duct of that thinking: the Babylonian Talmud. I am well
aware of the fact that this is a bold demand. But I do not
see how it can be avoided. It is highly improper that we,
or at least our leading representative circles, have no
inner relation to this work—a work to which we owe our
very unity and existence up to our own days. It may be
said, without exaggeration, that the majority of educated
Jews have never seen this work consciously even from
the outside. On the other hand, transmission of such general knowledge within twenty-five lessons—allowing forty
for the reading of the Bible and fifteen for a cursory
sketch of Jewish history—is not as hard as it appears at
first sight. The Hebrew language should by this time be
known so well that the Aramaic of the Talmud, supple-
mented by the Aramaic sections of the Bible, can be
treated as deviations from the Hebrew language. It will
then suffice to study some easy and yet characteristic texts
from different parts of this classical work. The student
will thereby gain an idea of the specifically talmudic
way of thinking, and an introductory concept of the
scope of the themes it discusses. Merely because the
Talmud is rather alien to our own way of thinking and
knowing, the difference between complete ignorance of
it and a superficial acquaintance is greater than that between superficial acquaintance and thorough familiarity.

Those who continue with their high school education
may, to a certain extent, be considered especially select;

whereas those who leave school at the age of fourteen or
fifteen may be considered the future guarantors of our
material existence. We shall now have to deal with the
former, with those who will exert their influence upon the
public opinion of the congregation or community. The
last three years, therefore, will be gauged more definitely
than before to the needs of future college graduates.

In the first of these three years the cursory contact with
the Talmud, gained in the preceding term, can be deep-
ened further. At the same time, talmudic literature in a
wider sense, especially the Midrashim, may be consulted
in order to regain access to the Jewish Year which had
been neglected during the previous year. A knowledge
of the Midrashim, which one might call a scientific
mythology, is necessary for the understanding of Jewish
thought. Besides this, so to speak, popular source of Jewish *Weltanschauung*, the time will have been reached for
a more thorough general view of its classical origin in
prophecy. To those individual prophetic chapters which
had previously been read, a thematic selection from
Amos and Hosea to Malachi and Daniel will be added.
During that time, approximately one half of that year
being used, it should be possible to study about one fifth
of the prophetic literature. If the quality of the material
selected is good, the quantity covered should be satisfactory. The prophetic portions of the Bible, representing
as they do the critical point and crossroads of religious
history, may now be used for a more thorough discussion
of our attitude to Christianity, a subject which had been
previously touched upon with less depth than is now
possible.

The foundation having been laid upon such rather

vast ground, makes possible in the succeeding year a
survey of the whole of the Exilic literature. The student
may be led from Philo[9] and Saadia[10] through Ibn Gabirol[11] and Ibn Ezra,[12] Judah ha-Levi[13] and Maimonides,[14]
Gersonides,[15] and Albo,[16] Joseph Karo,[17] and Moses
Isserles[18] and even up through Moses Mendelssohn and
Leopold Zunz,[19] and, according to the predilection of the
teacher, even further to our own times. Here, at last, we
have material which, to a great extent, may be taught in
translation; for the secret charm of the Hebrew word
has not been wrought at the cradle of most of these
works. Therefore a further translation into German will
not do much harm. Much can be pressed into such a
year. Eighty hours represent a long time for they cor-
respond to a college course of three hours through two
terms. Since a teacher, who, at this stage, feels the need
for giving tests and examinations is automatically dis-
qualified, the whole time available can be used for instruction and study. Greater depths must now follow upon
the widening of the view.

The last year of instruction should be dedicated mainly
to philosophy. Here the teacher's choice depends on his
own preferences. It is up to him whether to let his
students read part of the *Kuzari*,[20] the *Ikkarim*,[21] *The
Guide for the Perplexed*[22] or the *Duties of the Heart*;[23]
he may even be bold enough to allow them a glimpse into
the *Zohar*[24] or the Lurianic Kabbalah.[25] The impressive
wealth of the literature is not now so important as it was
in the preceding year. Gaining greater profundity at one
or more points is far more important. Many a teacher
may wish to read the *Book of Job* or *Ecclesiastes*. What
is important is that the future graduate shall gain strong

and lasting impressions, that he shall recognize Judaism not only as his own world, but also as a spiritual power to be guarded as such in his own life.

This is my plan. Although appealing at first sight, it is apparently beyond realization. The first reservation to be expressed concerns the fact that this project presupposes the existence of nine independent grades of instruction. This is indeed a *conditio sine qua non,* for every class must be taught by itself. The system—if system it can be called—of putting students together at different age levels, is the very death of inspired teaching. Teaching is based ideally on a constant and mutual relationship between the teacher and all of his students. If two thirds of the teacher's audience do not participate, they are dead weight for the good teacher who draws his inspiration from the very eyes of his disciples. This is not to mention the fact that saving a teacher's wages amounts under these conditions to wasting the students' time!

It should be relatively easy, however, to remedy the situation. All that is needed is to consolidate all the high school classes of the same age level of one city or school district. The amount of students in a class may reach thirty, but will be automatically reduced in the higher levels. The schools may be willing to set aside appropriate afternoon hours for this purpose.[26] Generally speaking, not being able to rely too much on the cooperation of the powers-that-be, we will have to use our own ingenuity. We cannot insist on having this instruction made obligatory, although this would be a desirable proof of our "equal rights." On the other hand, such an act would increase the intervention of the government in a measure not exactly beneficial for such a novel institution. Let us rather rely on our own material and educational resources to finance the undertaking and to interest students in joining. The authorities may object to seeing the Hebrew language become the center of Jewish religious instruction, although the study of Hebrew is not its aim, but rather a necessary means. They may also be afraid of overworking the students, a fear which is generally out of place, considering the "Jewish brains" of our children. And how much do two hours per week amount to if we compare them with the four or six hours per week devoted to music lessons and practice! There may be, however, other implicit objections not expressed here. For let us not be mistaken: it was precisely those liberal-minded Germans in charge of forming policy concerning Jews who worked under the assumption that emancipation will solve the Jewish question by leading to a kind of assimilation which even the most fervent assimilationist among us—as long as he wants to remain Jewish—will reject. Therefore we can only count on cautious support which even then will come from conservative circles rather than from liberal ones, although the conservatives misunderstand our reasons and our aims.

A similar method ought to be applied concerning the position of the teachers within the general staff. Here, as well, not too much energy should be wasted in a fight for equality. It is better to start from the bottom and to use our own resources; once we have erected an impressive structure, the authorities will act in their own interests by recognizing it officially and thus paving the way for their constant influence on it.

We have now reached the very core of the practical problem: the teachers. This is where the trouble lies, and the cure must be effected. This is not to say that we find fault with our Jewish primary school teachers. My own experiences and those of my childhood have made me respect their serious and not unsuccessful efforts in education; they have given a good account of themselves. Nevertheless, for reasons which do not wholly relate to education *per se* but still more to the interests of the Jewish community, it must be stated and it will be proven that the instruction we have in mind should, as far as feasible, be given by university graduates. It will not even be satisfactory to have high school teachers of mathematics or modern languages give this kind of instruction as an avocation. It is not only that after the war we could hardly count upon having sufficient high school teachers capable of taking charge of an instruction necessitating eighteen hours per week; but it is rather that we are in need of teachers with a thorough theological background. Not only the ministry, but education as well needs theologians who have gone through a scientific training.

It can hardly be denied that the type of the Western European rabbi is something new in Jewish history. Though we can still recognize the connection with the ancient tradition, more and more those features become visible which changed the scholar of old into the minister and, in liberal circles, even into the priest. We do not wish to criticize this development; new concepts are answering new requirements. What is fateful, however, is that the ancient concept has been discarded without seeing its survival guaranteed side by side with the new one. The most essential aspect of former times has vanished entirely: the old-time rabbi was, as in Eastern Europe he still is, unique in his congregation only as far as his office was concerned, but not in his scholarship, and certainly not in his way of life. Except for the administration of his office, he was, as a scholar, only one among others, most of the time among many others. He shared his scholarly degree with a good number of the members of his congregation, as is the case today with a Ph.D. But whereas the latter title does not stress any special group within the congregation, which the rabbi would be a member of because of that title, the title *Morenu* created, within the congregation, a group of Jewish scholars, and, within Jewry, the core of the public.

This kind of Jewish intelligentsia, corresponding to a secular one, is now missing. This lack is painfully conspicuous. Specific Jewish interests are no longer the concern of all, but the specialty of a very few. Jewish interests, wherever existent, relate to external affairs of the congregation and to the relationship to the State and to society, a relationship which does not touch on inner questions. The situation expresses itself in our Jewish periodicals as well. The lack of a common basis of understanding actually reflects the lack of which we spoke before, an intelligent public. A magazine, uniform in spite of the many voices expressed, does not exist in the Jewish community, and, owing to the present situation, it can not be created. How shallow are the literary societies and lodges that attempt to create and to strengthen such a Jewish public. You can not achieve a familiarity with your own Jewish milieu by lectures on "Judaism and—." We do not blame them for this, for they are trying something impossible. Neither lectures nor societies can reach this goal, as long as the foundation is missing: the school. This is sufficient to describe the problem of the public so far as it is engaged in the act of learning and is an agent of further development.

What about research? At this moment, one hundred years after the founder of the "Science of Judaism"[27] entered the university, this kind of Jewish literary research is being menaced by non-Jewish competition, which in any event had never respected it as an equal in the field of biblical research. From the general point of view of science this may or may not be a disaster yet for us it is dangerous. We do not have to go into details. One hundred years of Protestant treatment of the "Old Testament" speak for themselves. If modernized Christianity is to become the yardstick for "post-biblical Judaism" too, we can well imagine what is going to happen; the development of scholarly interests in Protestant theological circles is ripe for such a step. Scholars with great sagacity and erudition, but little understanding and sympathy for the peculiarities of Jewish religious thinking, will then apply their methods to Halakhah[28] and Aggadah,[29] to philosophy and Kabbalah, surprising us with the results of their inner criticism, as they have surprised us in the past with the separation in Psalm 72 of the supposedly inconsistent elements of "Jewish chauvinism" and "prophetic universalism," or with the elimination of the Suffering Servant from the great Messianic prophecy concerning the history of the Jewish people and all mankind (Isaiah 40 ff). In the special field which has so far been reserved for the Science of Judaism there are still enough phenomena which await the Protestant discovery of their "incompatibility." This is not to say that we do not admire the results of their research. The very mention of "Isaiah 40 ff" makes us their debtors, in spite of Ibn Ezra's hints. We do feel ashamed consequently to admit that our own studies of the Hebrew Bible have not produced anything of similar value, the more so since, in other fields, we have not been lacking in the spirit of independent research. At least, however, side by side with Protestant research we must gain a place for the Jewish position concerning these things, since they are of concern to our own family. Protestant research, too, will ultimately benefit from this variety of approach. However, the future does not immediately indicate any hope for such a development.

The reason for this hopelessness is the same as for the lack of an intelligent Jewish public: only future rabbis receive a theological education. This almost necessarily leads to an intellectual impoverishment or, at least, onesidedness. It is true that the Christian theological faculties of the universities, too, cater mainly to the needs of the ministry; but by their number alone they represent a structure of their own, a community of their own. Therefore in this community of scholars an independent spirit of scholarship could develop, aside from merely educational purposes. A similar situation could hardly be expected to arise within the confines of the Science of Judaism. For this reason research has always remained the concern of a few individual representatives

and has never created a school, through which the influence of their ideas could be secured for the future.
The vast number represented by Christian theological
faculties of the universities must therefore in our case
be replaced by something else. The demand we were
compelled to make regarding the improvement of religious instruction is now being repeated as a way leading
to the development of a satisfactory number of research
workers: the creation of a staff of teachers with a specifically theological training.

The training itself may not be so difficult; nevertheless,
how shall we pay such a staff, considering the financial
means at hand? The training could be done in the existing Rabbinical seminaries. Nevertheless, we should not
forget the aim of a Jewish-theological faculty in the
framework of a German university—the most important
thing we can now expect from the government, as long
as we foot the bill. Aside from the stimulating atmosphere
of life at a university, where the Jewish theologian would
pursue his studies, it would be an invaluable gain for
all of German Jewry to have an exalted scholarly representation in such a faculty. Interior difficulties should
not make this project impossible. The duplicity of religious "factions" could be bridged. All that is necessary
is to have two professorships for each subject, e.g., for
biblical, rabbinical, philosophical literature. The two
representatives will automatically treat different themes:
whereas the liberal biblical scholar will pursue criticism
of the Pentateuch, his orthodox colleague will speak on
the development of biblical exegesis; whereas the liberal
professor of rabbinical literature has chosen the Talmud
itself as his field of studies, his orthodox colleague will

read the Codes; whereas the liberal professor would lecture on systematic theology, the orthodox one will treat
the medieval period. Thus the division of labor would
be created automatically, because of the vastness of the
field. A not too small number of associate professors
would teach social and communal history as well as
Semitic languages, including not only talmudic Aramaic
but also some aspects of the Arabic language, for instance, philosophical terminology.

However, the orthodox-liberal juxtaposition is the only
one we have to recognize, as it has already been recognized in the administration of communal affairs. Our
time, however, knows of another one, overlapping with
the former: the contrast of the national and the religious
concept of Judaism. This dimension should however be
ignored, since it is mainly a political one. No question
should be asked about party affiliation. Our theological
faculty must be tolerant in this respect. Other difficulties,
arising from the relations towards our Rabbinical seminaries, must be overcome by good will. All these obstacles
should not be strong enough to make this infinitely important work impossible.

Even to secure the financial means from our own
resources should not be too hard. What remains doubtful,
however, is whether the government, in spite of the
friendly words expressed, would give its consent. Therefore this point in the present plan shall not be discussed
further; let us only count on the Rabbinical Seminaries
which are technically sufficient. To them we may entrust
the training of our teachers; they will have to adapt
themselves to this new task.

The important question that remains is: What next?

It is not enough for us to secure teachers trained in and by the Rabbinical Seminaries. As indicated before, we need not only teachers but over one hundred working scholars who, without being burdened by the duties of rabbinical office, would be able and willing to provide the Science of Judaism with that broad realm of possibilities it now requires. The teacher and the scholar must become one and the same person. His financial security, as well, must be based on both aspects of his work. We can fulfill this demand ourselves, without having to ask the government for support. I know that the amount required is by no means a small one, much more than would be needed to maintain a Jewish department at a university. What we need is no more and no less than this: an Academy for the Science of Judaism. Its blueprint must be so extended that existing plans are dwarfed by it. Its purpose is not only the organization of scientific research, for this by itself would allow us to start with small beginnings, since even a small achievement is an achievement after all. Its purpose is also the intellectual and material consolidation of the upper stratum of the teaching profession which involves at least one hundred and fifty scholars. Thus a fund is needed to supply one hundred and fifty stipends of about 2,500 marks each.[30] The recipient would be required to work on one of the projects of the Academy. Such projects would be directed by the members and, if there is a faculty, the members would belong to its staff. This staff would grow in relation to the increasing amount of its tasks. Otherwise this body of scholars must be drawn from the faculty of the Rabbinical Seminaries, and grow steadily by an election of new members.

The amount of money needed for this would be at least one million marks, or about the yearly budget of all the Jewish communities in Germany. One could indeed try to raise this amount by taxing all communities jointly for a one-time "educational contribution," to be paid up within three years. It would be a worthwhile secondary success if on this occasion all German-Jewish communities would be consolidated for a common purpose. Another method would be the one usually applied under similar circumstances: a collection. Foundations involving an original capital of between fifty and sixty thousand marks could be reserved for this purpose, and the publications financed by it should carry, on the title page, a note in whose memory the particular foundation was established.

The recipients of such stipends, although not required to do so, generally will seek a position as a teacher in the Jewish community. For eighteen hours of teaching per week the community will have to pay a salary which, though seeming exorbitant in comparison with the present wage scale, is not lavish when compared with what the state or the city pays their high school teachers. Were the congregation to pay 2,500 marks, such a teacher— scholar would earn 5,000 marks a year, which is an excellent income considering the fact that such positions can be filled before the middle twenties of one's life. Since the community, however, would benefit by such an unusually high teacher's salary, it is justified that it shall carry the financial burden, although somewhat mitigated by the fact that those parents who can afford to send their children through high school contribute most to the income of that community.

Let us try to picture what the position of the teacher-scholar involves.

The teacher-scholar will be on an equal footing with the rabbi, having received the same kind of theological training. But, unlike the average rabbi, his studies at the Academy will put him under the continuous and fruitful influence of an important scientific organization. Since his official duties are few, compared with those of a high school teacher, and occupy only the afternoon hours, he has much more time to spare for research. He will be less identified with the local staff than with a great scholarly body, comprising now only Germany but, depending on the possible development of a confederation of European States subsequent to the Peace Treaty, it may well extend over all of Central Europe. As a worker within such an Academy, he will organize lectures in the community, thereby infusing into their literary societies the fresh breath of a great scientific life. He will as well organize such affairs from time to time surrounding smaller communities. In the course of years his own disciples will form the nucleus of a spiritually alert public. Everywhere libraries will be established and supported by the communities, in the manner in which it is now being done in Berlin alone. Their reading rooms will attract many people. This could have been done for some time, since the means were there, but no interest was forthcoming. In many places all that is needed is the bringing together of the private collections scattered everywhere, the establishment of library hours with librarians, some of them on a voluntary basis, in charge of supervision and lending.

Such a teacher will also be able to represent to the

outside world the spiritual life of the community, in a more effective way than was possible, in most cases, for the rabbi. In those smaller cities which cannot boast of a university, he will be known as an Orientalist, and will thus "belong" to the small circle of local scholarly celebrities. Just because his activities are not limited to his official school duties, his position will rather be compared to that of the director of the Museum or Art Gallery or Public Library, or the high school teacher or minister who follows scholarly interests, or the director of the theatre or the conductor of the local orchestra. The teacher will inject into the internal and external concerns of the community a spirit of new life.

We need such a new spirit. At the beginning of the war many groups foresaw better times for the German Jews. This hope has been disappointed. If we take our Jewishness seriously, this is fortunate. Great and fateful changes should not come as a present; the times should not give us anything which we have not deserved by working for it. That merely external equality of rights which we had hoped for would have been just a gift. We would have attained as individuals what would have been denied to us as a community. There would have been no change in the status quo for German Jews. The only difference would have been that a benefit enjoyed so far only by a few, would now be shared by many, maybe even by a majority. But many individuals, even the sum total of all of them, are not the community. Sometimes it is a minority who represents a community better than a majority. It is the community which has to fight for equality of rights, and not only to fight for it, but to work for it. Once such an equality has been attained for

Jewry as a whole, it will subsequently also be gained
for individual Jews. However, the road towards equality
for the community leads through organization. Through
it the individual will be able to work consciously for the
spirit of the community.

When, in the first half of the last century, we were
invited to participate in the communal life of the people
and the State in Germany, this was done by removing,
for the individual, the barriers which up to that time
had prevented him from sharing such a life. True, the
individual who was to be emancipated was also surrounded by the barriers of his own communal life, but
this was at best considered a minor obstacle. If he were
only allowed to enter the gates of the great political
community of the German people, the fetters fastened
to the doors of his former spiritual and racial community would disappear by themselves. It was only the
reactionary who thought differently. The Jews' Laws,
planned by Frederic William IV, wanted to let the Jews
participate in the State, though not through the rights
newly granted to the individuals, but through a collective
constitution for Jewry. This was planned within the
framework of the political theory of those circles, which
tried to revitalize the collective fibers of the nation.
Applied to the Jews, however, who, in the preceding
decades had done a good job at re-educating themselves
by their own efforts, all the high-sounding philosophical
and political phrases could not but create the impression
that the clock was to be turned back. Therefore those
plans remained unsuccessful. No intelligent person among
us will wish to see them revived now. We even turn our
backs to those concepts regarding individual rights which

at least won for themselves a *de jure* recognition. We have learned that book laws are not sufficient for the individual. As long as the individual is emancipated and attracted only as an individual, by graciously overlooking the fact that he is a member of another community, the best he can gain for that community is a material success; from the point of view of inner life, however, it is not only no advantage for the community, but a loss. The community must be considered a community, to its own members as well as to the outside, otherwise, and in spite of our personal loyalty to it, the outside world will regard it at best as a more or less harmless blemish. The reactionaries of the middle of the 19th century wanted to create a body for Jewry. We want an organic representation of Judaism. We do not want to have organizations of Jews, but spiritually Jewish organizations. The spirit of Judaism must be planted and raised in institutions of its own. The problem of Jewish education, in every stage and in every form, is the task of the moment. Of the moment; for, verily, the time has come to work.

"It is time to work for the Lord;
They have made void Thy teachings."
(Psalm 119:126)

TOWARDS A RENNAISSANCE OF JEWISH LEARNING

To Eduard Strauss

The state of the world today may force us to postpone many desirable things, not for a better day but for a better century. It could hardly be asserted that the great urgency of the present moment is to organize the science of Judaism [*Wissenschaft des Judentums*] or to prompt both Jews and non-Jews to the endless writing of books on Jewish subjects. Books are not now the prime need of the day. But what we need more than ever, or at least as much as ever, are human beings—Jewish human beings, to use a catchword that should be cleansed of the partisan associations still clinging to it.

This term should not be taken in its (ostensibly loose) meaning, which is actually a very narrow one—it should not be taken in what I would call the petty-Jewish sense that has been assigned to it by exclusively political or even exclusively cultural Zionism. I mean it in a sense that though certainly including Zionism goes far beyond it. *The Jewish human being*—this does not mean a line drawn to separate us from other kinds of humanity. No dividing walls should rise here. A reality that only sheer stubbornness can deny shows that even within the individual many different spheres can touch or overlap. Yet sheer stubbornness and its counterpart, a cowardly renunciation, seem indeed to be the two main features of our present-day Jewish life.

When the problem is posed in terms of the extremist— of the Zionists and the assimilationists—the only solution is the either-or of stubbornness and repudiation. But the Jewishness of a Jew is done an injustice if it is put on the same level as his nationality. One nationality—the German, for instance—is of necessity differentiated from other nationalities. The German nationality of a Jew excludes his being simultaneously of French or British nationality. A German is after all only a German, not a Frenchman or an Englishman too. Significantly enough, language itself resists the use of the phrase "A German man." The relationship between a man's German nationality and his humanity is one that philosophers of history may meditate upon—and it may be the task of living, advancing history to realize this relationship—but there is no "relationship" between a man's Jewishness and his humanity that needs to be discovered, puzzled out, experienced, or created. Here the situation is different: As Jew he is a human being, as human being a Jew. One is a *jüdisch Kind* with every breath. It is something that courses through the arteries of our life, strongly or weakly, but at any rate to our very finger tips. It may course very weakly indeed. But one feels that the Jew in oneself is not a circumscribed territory bounded by other circumscribed territories, but a greater or lesser force flooding one's whole being.

Just as Jewishness does not know limitations inside the Jewish individual, so does it not limit that individual himself when he faces the outside world. On the contrary, it makes for his humanity. Strange as it may sound to the obtuse ears of the nationalist, being a Jew is no limiting barrier that cuts the Jew off from someone who is limited by being something else. The Jewish human being finds his limitation not in the Frenchman or German but only in another human being as unlimited as himself: the Christian or heathen. Only against them can he measure himself. Only in them does he find individuals who claim to be and are as all-embracing as himself, above and beyond all divisions of nationality and state, ability and character (for these too divide human beings from one another). His Judaism must, to the Jew, be no less comprehensive, no less all-pervasive, no less universal than Christianity is to the Christian human, or heathenism to the heathen humanist.

But how? Does not this mean the revival of that old song, already played to death a hundred years ago, about Judaism as a "religion," as a "creed," the old expedient of a century that tried to analyze the unity of the Jewish individual tidily into a "religion" for several hundred rabbis and a "creed" for several tens of thousands of respectable citizens? God keep us from putting that old cracked record on again—and was it ever intact? No, what we mean by Judaism, the Jewishness of the Jewish human being, is nothing that can be grasped in a "religious literature" or even in a "religious life"; nor can

it be "entered" as one's "creed" in the civil registry of
births, marriages, and deaths. The point is simply that
it is no entity, no subject among other subjects, no one
sphere of life among other spheres of life; it is not what
the century of emancipation with its cultural mania
wanted to reduce it to. It is something inside the individual that makes him a Jew, something infinitesimally
small yet immeasurably large, his most impenetrable
secret, yet evident in every gesture and every word—
especially in the most spontaneous of them. The Jewishness I mean is no "literature." It can be grasped through
neither the writing nor reading of books. It is not even—
may all the contemporary-minded forgive me!—"undergone." It is only lived—and perhaps not even that.
One *is* it.

One is Jewish. But of course Jewishness also exists in
itself. And because it exists, because it already is here
and was here before me and will remain when I am gone,
therefore—but *only* therefore—it is also literature. Only
for this reason are there problems of Jewish education.
Literature is written for the sake only of those who are
in process of development, and of that in each of us
which is still developing. Hebrew, knowing no word for
"reading" that does not mean "learning" as well, has
given this, the secret of all literature, away. For it is a
secret, though a quite open one, to these times of ours—
obsessed and suffocated as they are by education—that
books exist only to transmit that which has been achieved
to those who are still developing. While that which is
between the achieved and the developing, that which exists
today, at this moment—life itself—needs no books. If I
myself exist, why ask for something to "educate" me?

But children come and ask; and the child in myself awakes—the child that doesn't as yet "exist" and doesn't "live"—and it asks and wants to be educated and to develop—into what? Into something living, into something that exists. But just here is where an end is put to the making of books.

For life stands between two periods of time, in the moment between the past and the future. The living moment itself puts an end to the making of books. Only, right next to it are the realms of book-writing, that is, the two realms of culture. In neither realm does the making of books ever come to an end. No end is ever reached in the exploration of the past, where the moment means nothing until it has been pinned down in the showcase of the past, by those who seek in the future only what can be imagined in terms of the past. And there is no end to the teaching of the coming generation by those who use the moment only for the purpose of opening by their own ardor the unawakened souls of the young, and who take from the past only what is teachable, only that which can find a place in the unlocked souls of the new generation. There is no end to learning, no end to education. Between these two burns the flame of the day, nourished by the limited fuel of the moment; but without its fire the future would remain sealed and without its illumination the past would remain invisible.

Jewish study and teaching, Jewish learning and education—they are dying out among us. This assertion may offend many ears, but in making it I feel myself one with the best among the young, and among the old too—thank goodness for the last, for otherwise I should not feel sure of myself. Since the time of Moses Mendelssohn and Leopold Zunz our Jewish learning no longer has the courage to be itself, but instead runs at a respectful distance behind the learning of the "others." At a respectful distance—what others find an old story is so readily marveled at among ourselves as the very latest thing—at least by the small (and rightly so) circle of those who still pay any attention at all to this dance of shadows. What the sparrows chirp from the rooftops of intellectual Germany, still seems terrible heresy to us. Leaving the old ghetto, we have very quickly locked ourselves up in a new one. Only this time we do not want to admit it to ourselves. And this time we occupy ourselves with a learning that is just as little German and just as little Jewish as—well, as, for example, the "German" surnames our grandfathers adopted in the first dizziness of emancipation.

The situation is no better with respect to teaching. The trend toward conversion which every year takes away the best from among us, and not—as is so often and falsely asserted—the worst, can be blamed on our religious instruction. Max Brod's[1] verses on this subject in his great poem "To the Baptized Jews" are as true as prose. Certainly the individual is usually guiltless. Everything is connected with everything else in these matters. We have no teachers because we have no teaching profession; we have no teaching profession because we have no scholars; and we have no scholars because we have no learning. Teaching and study have both deteriorated. And they have done so because we lack that which gives animation to both science and education—life itself.

Life. A void, unfilled for ever a century, yawns between the two realms of culture with all the endless making of books that goes on in them. Emancipated Jewry
lacks a platform of Jewish life upon which the bookless
present can come into its own. Up to the time of emancipation, such a platform was provided by existence within
the bounds of old Jewish law and in the Jewish home and
synagogal service. Emancipation shattered this platform.
True, all three parts exist still, but because they are now
only parts, they are no longer what they were when they
were joined together—the single platform of a real and
contemporaneously lived life, which learning and education had but to serve and from which they drew their
greatest strength.

Wherever the Law is still kept among Western Jewry
it is no longer a living "Jewishness," one that while
largely based on legal paragraphs, was taken naturally
and as a matter of course. This sort of Judaism has
acquired a polemical point that quite contrary to any
original intent—is turned, not against the outsider, but
mainly against the large majority of those within Jewry
who no longer keep the Law. Today the Law brings out
more conspicuously the difference between Jew and Jew
than between Jew and Gentile.

Just as the Law, wrenched from its unity with home
and worship, is no longer what it once was, so the two
other planks of the platform are not what they used to
be. And thus the Jewish home, wherever it is still maintained intact, is no longer the heart from which the blood-
stream of all Jewish life is pumped, and to which it
returns. Slowly but surely the home has lost its dominat-
ing position in Jewish existence. Life comes from outside

and makes its own demands. The Jewish home can and probably will try to assert itself against the outside world, but the most it can still do is maintain itself. The unity between home and occupation has been destroyed beyond hope; and even the strictest Jewish orthodoxy is forced to initiate its pupils in two different worlds of culture, and to exaggerate the quite new and positive importance of the opposition between Torah and *derekh eretz*,[2] which was of so little significance for the old Judaism. And thus the home has become at best but "one thing" in life, with "another thing" by the side of it, and *outside* it. That "other thing"—one's occupation, one's public activity—is no longer the natural radiation of the home into the outside world; it obeys requirements and laws of its own. The home no longer binds Jewish life into a unity.

And finally there is the synagogue. Thence at least a stream of Jewish life still seems to flow, and though it is pitifully thin it does trickle through the modern Jew even if it does not wash over and around him. The most assimilated assimilationist does as a rule still take some part in its life, be it but for an hour's memorial service, or for his marriage, or at least for his funeral. Those who know and have perhaps experienced personally what forces still slumber in a mere Yom Kippur Jewishness—which many have held on to as the only coin, in an inherited fortune, that still retains its full value—will be careful not to speak disparagingly of the synagogue. But for the same reason that the Jewish home and Law cannot become what they once were, the synagogue cannot become what it once was for our collective existence.

Even if it were possible—and I think it is!—gradually to restore the synagogue's connection with the whole of

life out of the small remnant of it which is all that many
of us have left, the restored connection would be with a
whole that is no longer a whole. For the synagogue no
longer acts as a member completing the body of a living
life. The beadle no longer knocks at house doors to sum-
mon us to *shul*. How many synagogues still have a study
room with the heavy folios of the Talmud and its commentaries right next to the room of worship? The synagogue has become, quite in keeping with the spirit of
the culture-obsessed, pigeonholing nineteenth century, a
"place of religious edification" (or at least it claims to
have become this). "Religion," to which life has denied
a real place—and rightly, for life rightly rejects such
lifeless, partial demands—seeks a safe, and quiet little
corner. And it is indeed a little corner: life flows past
it unconcerned. Nor can the synagogue, either, do what
the Law and the home cannot—give Jewry a platform of
Jewish life.

What, then, holds or has held us together since the
dawn of emancipation? In what does the community of
our contemporary life show itself, that community which
alone can lead from the past to a living future? The
answer is frightening. Since the beginning of emancipation only one thing has unified the German Jews in a
so-called "Jewish life"; emancipation itself, the Jewish
struggle for equal rights. This alone covers all German
Jews, and this alone covers Jews only. From this alone,
therefore, those contemporary impulses will have to come
which will open up the past to the seeking eyes of the
student, and open the future to the capacity for leader-
ship of a determined will. Everyone knows what the true
situation is. Here, really, is the final reason why our

Jewish scholarship and our Jewish education are in such a bad way. This struggle for equal rights—civil as well as social—has been the only actual "stimulant" our scholarship and our education have got from real life. Which is why neither the one nor the other has been able to free itself from the blinkers of apologetics. Instead of feeling and teaching the enjoyment of that which is ours, and which characterizes us, they have again and again tried but to excuse it. And so we have come to our present pass.

Zionism, diagnostician of genius but most mediocre healer, has recognized the disease but prescribed the wrong treatment. What is recognized was the absence of a specific contemporary Jewish life having some common characteristics other than just the common possession of a dead scholarship called the "Science of Judaism" (which nobody is familiar with) and the common "defense against anti-Semitism." What Zionism also recognized—and here is proved itself to be a real pathologist, not merely a diagnostician—is this: that the only healthy, the only whole thing about the Jewish person—is the Jewish person himself.

Expressly or unconsciously, Zionism has always emphasized that it is the integrity of the Jewish individual which has in reality held us together since the beginning, and offered the only solid ground upon which the several vessels of Jewish life could develop—land, state, and law in the old days; later, divine commandment, worship, and home. But as soon as the great question is posed as to what should be done now, and how new vessels of Jewish communal life are to be planted in this devastated but indestructible soil in place of the shrunken ones, so that, grafting themselves on to these new vessels, individuals can again feel the sap of the old, eternally inexhaustible stream course through their arteries—as soon as this question is asked, Zionism fails us . . .

Those who want to work for the movement, for today, without shifting the main burden to an uncertain tomorrow, must take the Jewish individual seriously, here and now, as he is in his wholeness.

But how is this to be done? By beginning modestly— the only way one can begin with very large things that, one feels sure, must be all-inclusive, or else have no existence. What is intended to be of limited scope can be carried out according to a limited, clearly outlined plan—it can be "organized." The unlimited cannot be attained by organization. That which is distant can be reached only through that which is nearest at the moment. Any "plan" is wrong to begin with—simply because it is a plan. The highest things cannot be planned; for them, readiness is everything. Readiness is the one thing we can offer to the Jewish individual within us, the individual we aim at. Only the first gentle push of the will— and "will" is almost too strong a word—that first quite gentle push we give ourselves when in the confusion of the world we once quietly say, "we Jews," and by that expression commit ourselves for the first time to the eternal pledge that, according to an old saying, makes every Jew responsible for every other Jew. Nothing more is assumed than the simple resolve to say once. "Nothing Jewish is alien to me"—and this is in itself hardly a resolve, scarcely anything more than a small impulse to look around oneself and into oneself. What each will then see no one can venture to predict.

I will dare to predict only this much: that each will see the whole. For just as it is impossible to attain to the whole without modestly beginning with that which is nearest, so it is impossible for a person not to attain to the whole, the whole that is destined for him, if he has really found the strength to make that first simple and most modest beginning. It is necessary for him to free himself from those stupid claims that would impose Juda-"ism" on him as a canon of definite, circumscribed "Jewish duties" (vulgar orthodoxy), or "Jewish tasks" (vulgar Zionism), or—God forbid—"Jewish ideas" (vulgar liberalism). If he has prepared himself quite simply to have everything that happens to him, inwardly and outwardly, happen to him in a *Jewish way*—his vocation, his nationality, his marriage, and even, if that has to be, his Juda-"ism"—then he may be certain that with the simple assumption of that infinite "pledge" he will become in reality "wholly Jewish."

And there is indeed no other way to become completely Jewish; the Jewish human being arises in no other way. All recipes, whether Zionist, orthodox, or liberal, produce caricatures of men, that become more ridiculous the more closely the recipes are followed. And a caricature of a man is also a caricature of a Jew; for as a Jew one cannot separate the one from the other. There is one recipe alone that can make a person Jewish and hence—because he is a Jew and destined to a Jewish life—a full human being: that recipe is to have no recipe, as I have just tried to show in, I feel, rather inadequate words. Our fathers had a beautiful word for it that says everything: confidence.

Confidence is the word for a state of readiness that does not ask for recipes, and does not mouth perpetually,

"What shall I do then?" and "How can I do that?" Confidence is not afraid of the day after tomorrow. It lives in the present, it crosses recklessly the threshold leading from today into tomorrow. Confidence knows only that which is nearest, and therefore it possesses the whole. Confidence walks straight ahead. And yet the street that loses itself in infinity for the fearful, rounds itself imperceptibly into a measurable and yet infinite circle for those who have confidence.

Thus the Jewish individual needs nothing but readiness. Those who would help him can give him nothing but the empty forms of preparedness, which he himself and only he may fill. Who gives him more gives him less. Only the empty vessels in which something can happen may be kept in readiness—"time" and "space." Really nothing more is needed—time to speak in, and space to speak in. This is all that can be "organized" in advance, and it is very little—next to nothing.

Our new Jewish periodicals, which in recent years have taken on more and more of the character of open forums, have sensed this need very subtly. Thus they, and especially Buber's *Der Jude*, which is the best among them, have become real forces in our life, perhaps even the most vital. The "Jewish adult education movement" [*Volkshochschul-Bewegung*]—a bad designation because it suggests an incorrect parallel with the movement for German adult education with its quite different aims—is the latest and perhaps most important movement among contemporary German Jews. But it must make clear to itself what it intends to do. Exploiting the big-city public's insatiable hunger for lectures, it can fill the enormous gaps in Jewish education by supplying what "religious" instruction neglected and what the universities failed to offer. It would probably have to offer as complete a series of courses as possible, a curriculum as encyclopedic as possible—in other words, an education. Given things as they are, however, and despite the best of intentions— which this movement, in contrast to our degenerated system of religious instruction, certainly has—it would become merely a substitute in the long run for something that should normally be offered elsewhere but cannot because the living force, the center and germ cell of a Jewish life, is wanting. Only in such a life the endless book world of education could find its end; here, too, a new, bookless, start could be made.

But the movement in question might try to become this very center of a Jewish life. It might try to become the form for such a life, but certainly only the first, empty, immediate form. It would try to be a beginning. Instead of confronting the seeker of knowledge with a planned whole, to be entered step by step, it would keep itself a mere modest beginning, the mere opportunity to make a beginning. At a university the student is faced with the edifice of a science that is complete in general outline and only needs development in detail; it lies outside the student, and he must enter it and make himself at home in it. This movement, however, would begin with its own bare beginnings, which would be simply a space to speak in and time in which to speak.

Nothing more? Yes, nothing more. Have "confidence" for once. Renounce all plans. Wait. People will appear who prove by the very fact of their coming to the discussion room of a school of Jewish adult education (will

someone suggest a better word?) that the Jewish human
being is alive in them. Otherwise, they would not come.
To begin with, don't offer them anything. Listen. And
words will come to the listener, and they will join together and form desires. And desires are the messengers
of confidence. Desire that join and men that join together:
Jews—and an attempt is made to supply them with what
they ask for. This too will be done modestly. For who
knows whether desires such as these—real, spontaneous
desires, not artificially nurtured by some scheme of education—can be satisfied? But those who know how to
listen to real wishes may also know perhaps how to point
out the desired way. This will be the hardest task of all.
For the teacher able to satisfy such spontaneous desires
cannot be a teacher according to a plan; he must be much
more and much less, a master and at the same time a
pupil. It will not be enough that he himself knows or that
he himself can teach. He must be capable of something
quite different—he himself must be able to "desire." He
who can desire must be the teacher here. The teachers
will be discovered in the same discussion room and the
same discussion period as the students. And in the same
discussion hour the same person may be heard as both
master and student. In fact, only when this happens will
it become certain that a person is qualified to teach.

It is essential that the discussion place be a single
room—without a waiting room. The discussion must be
"public." Those who come can wait in the discussion room
itself. They can wait until the moment comes for them to
join in. The discussion should become a conversation.
Anyone who wants to continue the conversation with a
single person can make an appointment for some later

time. The discussion period should bring everybody together. For it brings people to each other on the basis
of what they all have in common—the consciousness, no
matter how rudimentary, no matter how obscured or con-
cealed, of being a Jewish human being. That one can meet
others on such a basis, that one can desire in common
with others—this will be an experience, even if the desire
remains unsatisfied. And this should be allowed for. Just
as a lecture might not be given for want of an audience,
so a desire may go unsatisfied for want of a teacher. This
does not matter. The lecture that is announced but never
given remains stillborn because it remains the intention
of but a single person; a common wish, however, that goes
unsatisfied stays alive because it unites many.

With the discussion period open to the public, we are
assured of this. The public aspect is not propitious to that
mortal adversary who dogs the steps of our German
Jewry—especially, let it be said, of its non-Zionist elements—the "stuffed shirt." All the "stuffed shirts" and
those who aspire to become "stuffed shirts," all these
young and old cases of senility, simply won't dare to
enter the discussion room. Questions are asked there, but
they want proclamations. Doubts are entertained there,
but they want programs. Desires are expressed there, but
they want demands. It is as unlikely that "stuffed shirts"
will stray in among these students—unless they see the
light and shed their starched shirt fronts—as it is that
the lions of the lecture-platform will be heard among
their teachers. There has been enough of speechmaking.
The speaker's platform has been perverted into a false
pulpit long enough among us—just punishment for a
rabbinate that, for the most part, has been able at best

to convert the pulpit into a speaker's platform. The voices
of those who want these desirous students to desire them
as teachers must lose the "true ring" of dead-sure conviction. For those who haven't had more than enough of
this ring will hardly find their way to us.

But who else will? I can already hear voices saying:
"How vague, how undefined, how cloudy." Let those who
talk this way remain in the realm of the certain, the definite, in the bright light of the commonplaceness in which
they feel so comfortable. It would be of little use to add
to the sobriety they already possess an equally sober and
ordinary "Judaism"—which is all they will get if they
ask this way.

I can also hear the voices of those who say: "How
little." Let those who talk this way remain undisturbed
amid the "much" they possess. For it would be of little
use to add to their collection of so many different things
another little knickknack labeled: "my Jewishness"—
which is all they will get if they ask this way.

But perhaps here and there someone will say longingly,
"How beautiful," and think hesitantly, "If such a thing
only existed—" I grant the doubts of such as *these*. Let
them doubt, but let them come. Let them find out whether
"such a thing exists." It depends on them and only on
them whether it does exist. It depends on their power to
wish, their urge to question, their courage to doubt.
Among *them* are the students and the masters. Let them
come. If they do not come, then Ecclesiastes is right for
our generation too: of the making of many books there is
no end.

THE BUILDERS:

Concerning the Law

> And all thy children shall be taught of the Lord, and great shall be the peace of thy children! (ISAIAH, 54: 13). Do not read 'banayikh', thy children, but 'bonayikh', thy builders.

To Martin Buber

Dear Friend:

When reading your Lectures about Judaism,[1] covering a whole decade and now contained in a little volume, I am amazed to see to what degree you have become the representative speaker and the advocate of our generations, mine as well as the one after me. We may have forgotten this at times, in the heat of the battle into which your thoughts dragged us when reading your Lectures for the first time; now that we re-read them with calm, and yet not too objectively but with, so to say, autobiographical excitement, we see clearly that it was our own words to which you were the first to give expression.

The preface shows that you had the same experience: When you collected the eight Lectures you were seized by feelings of autobiographical retrospect; not in the sense of a merely historical review—for this neither you nor the Lectures are prepared. But in the sense of an examination of your own past in the light of the present and the future. You know how closely connected I feel to the writer of that preface. When I read it for the first time, a few months ago, I had accepted your assurance that the present state of your knowledge, from which you had looked back on the road of the past, had meant for you clarification, not conversion. Now, when I read these words again, and go over your lectures once more, I understand how you, and only you, can say that. For a word does not remain its speaker's possession; he to whom it is addressed, he who hears it, or acquires it by chance—they all get a share of it; the word's fate, while in their possession, is more fate-ful than what its original speaker experienced when first uttering it. And the words of the preface must convey conversion, and not only clarification, to those who read or hear the Lectures. For you they meant only clarification, for you have remained the same; but your words have really gone through the experience of a change of heart: they have been changed.

Now that your words have stepped into the clarity of the immediate speech; now that you do not have to conjure the Spirit any more, when you wish to call by name the One Who is Spirit, but only insofar as He "is," and Who wants to be named the way He can be addressed— for "as His name, so is His praise"—you speak now to other hearers, even though they are the same as the ones who listened to you before. For if your new words are to be understood, other chords must vibrate in the souls of your listeners. And only he can become your listener who like yourself can commit himself to an unmediated relationship to things. New listeners, however, always imply new demands; thus a teacher himself is changed by what

he teaches his students; or, at least he must be prepared
to have his words changed, if not himself.

You know the problem I have at heart. Your eight lectures touch on it over and over, and the eighth[2] finally
moves it into the foreground. In the earlier lectures, the
problem of Jewish law and practice is broached really
only for the sake of completeness. In the final two we
feel that it has gained in urgency; if not for yourself,
then certainly for your audience. Ultimately it joins with
its twin problem, Jewish teachings; and the question:
"What shall we do?" attaches to both a very real and
immediate interest. But while the problem of teachings
has heretofore gone through a visible development which
has posed the question fully ripened at the precise moment of the answer, the question of the Law would seem
in 1919 to be formulated much as it was in 1909. Because
of the contrast, I make bold once again to present for
revision the old solution. And even if here and now you
can clarify the problem in theory only—that too will be
of value. For that matter, what I myself have to say about
it is not based on the experience of having reached the
goal but on that of seeking and being on the way.

The development that, to my mind, your conception of
the teachings has undergone, unfolds in what you call
"invisible Judaism." Originally this is treated as a solid
concept; something like prophecy versus legalism, or
hasidism versus rabbinic opposition. In subsequent lectures, however—or am I mistaken?—it comes to resemble
an intricate river system, in which the waters above
ground seem everywhere to accompany those in subter-
ranean depths. But in the final lecture, in the blazing light
of the question that converts the problem into something

actual, the picture changes; the visible streams and those underground are no longer distinguishable from one another, and whether those deeper tides are ever reached depends only on the hand that dips down to take. For you have formulated the goals of our Jewish learning in such a way that nothing Jewish may be excluded as alien. The distinctions between "essential" and "nonessential" which were forced upon us throughout the nineteenth century no longer hold. Now we must learn to recognize the hidden essence in the "nonessential"; and to accept the "essential" as we face it in the realities of Jewish life, where it turns out to be of the same shape as the "nonessential": indeed, often deriving its shape from the latter.

Apparently then, the essential and the nonessential merge so wholly in this learning that the recurring "this too!" dissolves all those inner differences which liberalism insisted on championing, and previous to liberalism, the ethical and philosophical movements of earlier centuries.

But now you point to a new principle of selection, through which the vast subject matter of learning [Lernstoff] you unfurl can again become a teaching [Lehre], a principle more trustworthy than anyone has attempted to set up. You introduce the concept of inner power. For inner power is what you demand when you ask him who learns to stake his whole being for the learning, to make himself a link in the chain of tradition and thus become a chooser, not through his will but through his ability. We accept as teaching what enters us from out of the accumulated knowledge of the centuries in its apparent and, above all, in its real contradictions. We do not know in advance what is and is not Jewish teaching;

when someone tries to tell us, we turn away in unbelief
and anger. We discern in the story of Hillel and the
heathen,[3] quoted *ad nauseam,* the smiling mockery of the
sage, and it is not to his first words that we adhere, but
to his final word: go and learn.

But in this wise, the teaching ceases to be something
that can be learned, something "knowable" in the sense
that it is an already existing "something," some definite
subject matter. The subject matter must indeed be learned
and known, and in a far wider sense than either the representatives of "Judaism on one foot" or those of traditional erudition and learning ever demanded. For now
the outside books,"[4] the books from beyond the pale, and
the "women's books" that were considered beneath the
dignity of that classical form of learning, are both included in the subject matter to be learned, included as
equals. But all this that can and should be known is not
really knowledge! All this that can and should be taught
is not teaching! Teaching begins where the subject matter
ceases to be subject matter and changes into inner
power . . .

The *way* to the teaching leads through what is "knowable"; at least that is the high road, the sole road one can
in good faith recommend to every questioner; in good
faith and even in the well-founded hope that he will find
it. But the teaching itself is not knowable. It is always
something that is in the future, and he who asks for it
today in his very question may offer a partial answer
to be given someone else tomorrow, and certainly affords
the larger part of the answer to be given today to the
questioner himself.

Earlier centuries had already reduced the teachings to

a genteel poverty, to a few fundamental concepts; it remained for the nineteenth to pursue this as a consistent method, with the utmost seriousness. You have liberated the teaching from this circumscribed sphere and, in so doing, removed us from the imminent danger of making our spiritual Judaism depend on whether or not it was possible for us to be followers of Kant.

And so it is all the more curious that after liberating us and pointing the way to a new teaching, your answer to the other side of the question, the question concerning the Law: "What are we to do?"—that your answer should leave this Law in the shackles put upon it—as well as upon the teachings—by the nineteenth century. For is it really Jewish law with which you try to come to terms? and, not succeeding, on which you turn your back only to tell yourself and us who look to you for answer that our sole task must be to take cognizance of the Law with reverence—a reverence which can effect no practical difference in our lives or to our persons? Is that really Jewish law, the law of millennia, studied and lived, analyzed and rhapsodized, the law of everyday and of the day of death, petty and yet sublime, sober and yet woven in legend; a law which knows both the fire of the Sabbath candle and that of the martyr's stake? The law Akiba[5] planted and fenced in, and Aher[6] trampled under, the cradle Spinoza hailed from, the ladder on which the Baal Shem[7] ascended, the law that always rises beyond itself, that can never be reached—and yet has always the possibility of becoming Jewish life, of being expressed in Jewish faces? Is the Law you speak of not rather the Law of the Western orthodoxy of the past century?

Here too, to be sure, the limiting process of reducing

to formulas was not initiated in the nineteenth century.
Just as the formulas into which the liberalism of the re-
formers wanted to crowd the Jewish spirit can be traced
back to a long time of antecedents, so too can one trace
back the reasons that S. R. Hirsch[8] gives to his *Yisroel-
Mensch* for keeping the Law. But no one before Hirsch
and his followers ever seriously attempted to construct
Jewish life on the narrow base of these reasons. For did
any Jew prior to this really think—without having the
question put to him—that he was keeping the Law, and
the Law him, only because God imposed it upon Israel at
Sinai? Actually faced by the question, he might have
thought of such an answer; and the philosophers to whom
the question has been put because they were supposedly
"professional" thinkers, have always been fond of giving
this very reply.

From Mendelssohn on, our entire people has subjected
itself to the torture of this embarrassing questioning; the
Jewishness of every individual has squirmed on the
needle point of a "why." Certainly, it was high time for
an architect to come and convert this foundation into a
wall behind which the people, pressed with questions,
could seek shelter. But for those living without questions,
this reason for keeping the Law was only one among
others and probably not the most cogent. No doubt the
Torah, both written and oral was given Moses on Sinai
but was it not created before the creation of the world?[9]
Written against a background of shining fire in letters of
somber flame? And was not the world created for its
sake? And did not Adam's son Seth found the first House
of Study for the teaching of the Torah? And did not the
patriarchs keep the Law for half a millennium before

Sinai? And—when it was finally given on Sinai—was it not given in all the seventy languages spoken in the world? It has 613 commandments, a number which, to begin with, mocks all endeavor to count what is countless, but a number which is in itself (plus the two command: ments heard directly from the lips of the Almighty) represents the numerical value of the word Torah and the sum of the days of the year and the joints in the body of man. Did not these 613 commandments of the Torah include everything that the scrutiny and penetration of later scholars, who "put to shame" our teacher Moses himself, discovered in the crownlets and tips of the letters? And everything that the industrious student could ever hope to discover there, in all future time? The Torah, which God himself learns day after day!

And can we really fancy that Israel kept this Law, this Torah, only because of the one "fact which excluded the possibility of delusions," that the six hundred thousand heard the voice of God on Sinai?[10] This "fact" certainly does play a part, but no greater part than all we have mentioned before, and all that our ancestors perceived in every "today" of the Torah: that the souls of all generations to come stood on Sinai along with those six hundred thousand, and heard what they heard. For a Jewish consciousness that does not question and is not questioned, all this is as important as the "fact," and that "fact" no whit more important than these other considerations.

The "only" of orthodoxy should no more frighten us away from the Law than the "only" of liberalism, once you had taught us to see, could block our way to the *teaching*. Judaism includes these "onlies," but not in the sense of "onlies." The problem of the Law cannot be dispatched by merely affirming or denying the pseudo-historical theory of its origin, or the pseudo-juristic theory of its power to obligate, theories which Hirsch's orthodoxy made the foundation of a rigid and narrow structure, unbeautiful despite its magnificence. Similarly as with teaching which cannot be dispatched by affirming or denying the pseudological theory of the unity of God of the pseudo-ethical theory of the love of one's neighbor, with which Geiger's[11] liberalism painted the façade of the new business or apartment house of emancipated Jewry. These are pseudo-historical, pseudo-juristic, pseudo-logical, pseudo-ethical motives: for a miracle does not constitute history, a people is not a juridical fact, martyrdom is not an arithmetical problem, and love is not social. We can reach both the teachings and the Law only by realizing that we are still on the first lap of the way, and by taking every step upon it, ourselves. But what is this way to the Law?

What was it in the case of the teachings? It was a way that led through the entire realm of the knowable, but really *through* it; a way that was not content to touch upon a few heights which yielded a fine view, but struggled along where former eras had not thought it even worth while to blaze a trail and yet would not give him who had traveled its whole length the right to say that he had now arrived at the goal. Even such a one could say no more than that he had gone the whole way but that even for him the goal lay a step beyond—in pathlessness. Then why call it a way—a path? Does a path—any path—lead to pathlessness? What advantage has he who has gone the way over him who right at the outset ventured the leap, which must come in the end in any case? A very small advantage, which most people do not consider worth so much trouble, but which, we believe, justifies the utmost trouble; for only this laborious and aimless detour through knowable Judaism gives us the certainty that the ultimate leap, from that which we know to that which we need to know at any price, the leap to the teachings, leads to *Jewish* teachings.

Other nations do not feel this kind of need. When a member of one of the nations teaches, he is teaching out from amongst his people and toward his people, even if he has learned nothing. All he teaches becomes the possession of his people. For the nations have a face still in the making—each its own. None of them knows at birth just what it is to be; their faces are not molded while they are still in nature's lap.

But our people, the only one that did not originate from the womb of nature that bears nations, but—and this is unheard of!—was led forth "a nation from the midst of another nation" (Deuteronomy 4:34)—our people was decreed a different fate. Its very birth became the great moment of its life, its mere being already harbored its destiny. Even "before it was formed," it was "known," like Jeremiah its prophet. And so only he who remembers this determining origin can belong to it; while he who no longer can or will utter the new word he has to say "in the name of the original speaker," who refuses to be a link in the golden chain, no longer belongs to his people. And that is why this people must learn what is knowable as a condition for learning what is unknown, for making it his own.

All this holds also for the Law, for doing. Except that what is doable and even what is not doable yet must be done nonetheless, cannot be known like knowledge, but can only be done. But if, for the time being, we set aside this grave difference, the picture is the same. There the way led through all that is knowable; here it leads through all that is doable. And the sphere of "what can be done" extends far beyond the sphere of the duties assumed by orthodoxy. As in the *teaching,* the rigid difference between the essential and the non-essential, as outlined by liberalism, should no longer exist, so in the sphere of what can be done the difference between the forbidden and the permissible, as worked out, not without precedent, yet now for the first time with so much consequence and efficiency by Western European orthodoxy of the 19th century, must cease to exist. The separation of the forbidden from the permissible had instituted a Jewish sphere within one's life; whatever remained outside of this sphere, whatever was extra-Jewish, was released, or, in legal terms, was made "permissible";[12] whatever remained within constituted the Jewish sphere with its commandments and prohibitions. The method of basing "allowances" on the text of the law permitted an extension of the realm of the permissible as long as the norms valid for the inner sphere were observed; this procedure, recognized through the ages as legitimate, had only in modern times been made into a system. Only in earlier periods where the security of Jewish life had been at stake, had that boundary been recognized and its temporary extension been accepted as its necessary complement. Only in modern times, when Jewish survival was considered perpetually at stake, was this treatment of the law given a permanent status. The future must no longer recognize that boundary, that method, nor even the general distinction described above. As in the sphere of the Law, there should be nothing *a priori* "permissible." Exactly those things, generally rendered permissible by orthodoxy, must be given a Jewish form. Outside of the Jewish sphere is the domain that should be formed by the "custom," i.e., by a positive principle, instead of merely the negative concept of "permissible." Where Judaism was alive, this had always been true; but whereas previously this fact had been treated with criticism or with slight irony, it will in the future have to be treated with seriousness. Not one sphere of life ought to be surrendered. To give one example for each of the two possibilities I have in mind: for those who eat Jewish dishes all the traditional customs of the menu as handed down from mother to daughter must be as irreplaceable as the separation of meat and milk; and he who refrains from opening a business letter on the Sabbath must not read it even if somebody else has opened it for him. Everywhere the custom and the original intention of the law must have the same rank of inviolability as the law itself.

Even what is within that sphere of demarcations, within that inner realm of Judaism, will be influenced by the fact that it is no longer separated from the realm of the merely "permissible." By contrast to the "permissible" it was essentially a sphere dominated by the term "forbidden." Even the positive commandment had somehow received a negative character. The classical Hebrew term for fulfilling one's duty, an expression which may be rendered by "discharging one's obligation," had a fateful implication, which it could not have where leaving the sphere of one obligation meant entering the sphere of another—an implication which, however, it had to adopt when all around the province of the Jewish duty lay the domain of a Jewishly formless "permissible." As in the sphere of *teaching* where, after the non-essential has become essential, the essential itself receives some of the characteristics of the non-essential; so in the sphere of the Law, after customs have clothed themselves with the dignity of law, the law will share the positive character of the custom. Not the negative but the positive will be dominant in the Law. Even the prohibitions may now reveal their positive character. One refrains from working on the Sabbath because of the positive commandment concerning rest; when refraining from eating forbidden food one experiences the joy of being able to be Jewish even in the every-day and generally human aspects of one's material existence. Even an act of refraining becomes a positive act.

Thus the demarcation line is broken: the two worlds, the one of the Jewishly forbidden and the one of the "permissible" extra-Jewish, flow into one another. The parallel arrangement of Jewish and extra-Jewish deeds disappears; in both spheres we meet naturally grown freedom. The sphere of possible activity, of the do-able, has become one. Herein is contained the form which (even in its injunctions) allows an experience of freedom. But freedom, in this sphere, even when it appears playful and unconcerned, must lead to form and to a Thou shalt! In this united sphere of the do-able lies, for instance, the legal exclusion of the woman from the religious congregation; but also in it lies with equal force her ruling rank in the home, given to her by age-old custom, and acknowledged by the husband on Friday evening in the biblical song of the Woman of Valour.[13] In this sphere lies the prohibition of images, again not realized according to what is being uprooted, but according to what is being planted and cared for: the sense of the incomparableness of the One, and not less the infinite and infinitely many-sided raiment of melodies which the course of the centuries has woven around the Invisible and His service. In it lies the rigid seclusion from the nations, which the Law enforces to the very details of every-day life, but again not realized in the manner of external isolation but, rather, in that of an internal union; and yet the historical law of assimilation lies in it as well, with none among the nations subjected to it so actively and so passively as the messianic people. Both aspects impose on us equal responsibility, restraining our energies, releasing new energies. The field of action is one.

And again we have to realize that with this unifying and broadening of the Jewishly do-able, nothing has really been done. Whatever can and must be done is not yet deed, whatever can and must be commanded is not yet commandment. Law [Gesetz] must again become commandment [Gebot] which seeks to be transformed into deed at the very moment it is heard. It must regain that living reality [Heutigkeit] in which all great Jewish periods have sensed the guarantee for its eternity. Like teaching, it must consciously start where its content stops being content and becomes inner power, our own inner power. Inner power which in turn is added to the substance of the law. For even if one should wish to do "everything" possible, he would still not fulfill the Law— he would not fulfill it in a way by which law would

become commandment; a commandment which he must
fulfil, simply because he cannot allow it to remain unful-
filled, as it was once expressed in Akiba's famous parable
of the fishes. Thus what counts here, too, is not our will
but our ability to act. Here too the decisive thing is the
selection which our ability—without regard to our will—
makes out of the wealth of the possible deeds. Since this
selection does not depend on the will but on our ability,
it is a very personal one; for while a general law can
address itself with its demands to the will, ability carries
in itself its own law; there is only my, your, his ability
and, built on them, ours; not everybody's. Therefore,
whether much is done, or little, or maybe nothing at all,
is immaterial in the face of the one and unavoidable
demand; that whatever is being done, shall come from
that inner power. As the knowledge of everything knowable is not yet wisdom, so the doing of everything do-able
is not yet deed. The deed is created at the boundary of
the merely do-able, where the voice of the commandment
causes the spark to leap from "I must" to "I can." The
Law is built on such commandments, and only on them.

The growth of the Law is thus entrusted once again to
our loving care. Nobody should be allowed to tell us
what belongs to its spheres, as nobody was allowed to
tell us what belonged to the sphere of teaching. We should
not even wish to know that beforehand, even if we could.
Neither our wish nor our knowledge should anticipate
that choice. We may know beforehand the sphere of the
do-able; we may wish beforehand that our deed shall
find its place within that sphere; but whether it will
actually find it there does not depend on our knowledge
or wish, however much we assign them direction and

location in the sphere. There is no other guarantee for our deed being Jewish, whether it will be found to lie within or beyond the precincts of the do-able. In the latter case the boundaries will be extended by them. In either case, however, it will be today's living law, as well as The Law. For this is what we felt was lacking in the law presented to us by its new observers: that the old law was not at the same time the new. This lack of actuality, of living reality, was recognized when the line of demarcation I mentioned made today's life "permissible." Thereby the law had been denied actuality. Moses' bold words, spoken to the generation who had not experienced the event of Mount Sinai (Deuteronomy 5:3), "The Lord made not this covenant with our fathers, but with us, even us, who are all of us here alive this day,"—those words (the paradox of which was keenly felt by ancient commentators) had fallen into oblivion. It is upon us to accept the challenge of this boldness. The inner line of demarcation has become blurred, and there must be an outer one, for not every deed which fails to find its place in the law known to us broadens its boundaries, as not every piece of our knowledge becomes a part of the *teaching*. But we cannot know whether it will not happen after all. We do not know the boundary, and we do not know how far the pegs of the tent of the Torah may be extended, nor which one of our deeds is destined to accomplish such widening. We may be sure that they are being extended through us; for could anything be allowed to remain outside permanently? If such were possible the boundary would assume a character it should not have; as rigid and as fixed as the distinction between the forbidden and the permissible, which had been discarded.

All of a sudden it would have turned again into an inner boundary, and our deeds would have been deprived of a most noble heritage: that, in the words of the Talmud, we have only to be sons, in order to become builders.

But does not this talmudic word with which we conclude every study meeting put to us the hardest question? Yes, to us, especially to us. For if we are not still sons, can we become sons again? Is not this the most pronounced difference between teaching and law: that we may well return to the former, for it is only the return of the consciousness, only the contemplation of one's self, but we cannot return to the latter, for it cannot be done in consciousness alone, but must be accomplished in the deed, and the deed cannot stand a return, it must always go forward; if it looks backwards, it does not experience deepening, as it is in the case of knowledge, but becomes a romantic enthusiasm or, to express it less courteously, a lie. It would even be the most dangerous of all lies— a lie in deed! A lie spoken can easily be repaired: you can take it back; but you cannot take back a deed. I do not wish to make this question appear less serious; it stood behind everything I have said so far. I do not believe in the harmlessness of a return in the case of consciousness. A mental pestilence like romanticism is not abolished by destroying its breeding ground. A lie spoken is as little revocable as a lie done. The road of the thought can as little turn back as the road of the deed. The thought, too, has to follow the law of progress. In the life of the spirit it is an exception if it is able to look back without harm, at the moment when it may even be wholesome for it to do so. Contemplation of one's self may lead to intellectual suicide. When is the return wholesome and when is it dangerous?

The life of the spirit runs its steady course, and in this process it discharges dead matter; only at this price is rejuvenation granted to it; every birth implies a death. This dead matter may be carried in the stream for a long time; only by accident may it be swept to the banks. Now, since not all the waves in the stream of the spirit move with the same speed—for some are well in advance while others are behind—it is in the interest of the whole if those in front stop from time to time and, looking back, wait for those left behind. The same applies to the self-contemplation of the individual and the cultural group. The danger of looking back is, however, that, although one waits for both, one fails to distinguish between the dead waste in the stream and those whose slower speed is due to their proximity to the source. Consequently that dead mass, believed alive, causes the stream to become stagnant. Therefore it is of the utmost importance for the spirit—both in the *vita contemplativa* as in the *vita activa*—whether it has the calm instinct to distinguish between those masses which are dead and those which are alive. The artificial rejuvenation of outmoded political institutions is not more dangerous than the rejuvenation of a dead faith. An example of the former are the midsummer night dreams of Frederic William IV concerning the German States, by comparison with the reconstitution in nineteenth century Europe of the court of assizes as it had been preserved in England. An example of the latter are the attempts in our own days to recreate in German nationalistic circles a belief in Woden by comparison with the renaissance of the world of fairy tales and folk legends in the nineteenth century.

Thus the danger for knowledge is no less than for doing; but the prospects too are the same. They lie in what I have just called the instinct for the difference between life and death. This instinct may err, but its errors are rarely ever fatal for the nations of the world, because in their history turning back is hardly ever of vital importance. With our people things are different. For our life does not run in one steady course like theirs. Our independence from history or, to put it positively, our eternity, gives simultaneity to all moments of our history. Turning back, recapturing what has remained behind, is here a permanent and life necessity. For we must be able to *live* in our eternity. The protecting wall of the instincts, sufficient for the nations of the world, who are endangered only occasionally, does not suffice for us. We need stronger safeguards than our instincts. These safeguards stem from what we found before to be ultimately decisive: the measure of our ability to act. Referring oneself to such a court of appeal is not flippancy, it is extremely serious when re-interpreting Israel's free acceptance of God's word "under" Mount Sinai into a compelled acceptance, compelled by—God. "He lifted up the mountain like a basket, until they accepted," the Sages say.[14] We may do what is in our power to remove obstacles; we can and should make free our ability and power to act. But the last choice is not within our will; it is entrusted to our ability.

It is true that ability means: not to be able to do otherwise—to be obliged to act. In our case, it is not up to an instinct, choosing by trial and error, to fight against the dangers of a return: our whole being is involved in it.

For this is what the appeal to ability means. As our whole being is at every moment placed before the task of returning home, not only certain layers and domains of being, as with the other nations; so also must the acceptance of the task be made by our whole being, not only certain moments of history, as with the nations of the world. A decision based on ability cannot err, since it is not choosing, but listening and therefore only accepting. For this reason no one can take another person to task, though he can and should teach him; because only *I* know what *I* can do; only my own ear can hear the voice of my own being which I have to reckon with. And perhaps another's non-ability does more for the upbuilding of both teaching and law than my own ability. We only know that we all have potential abilities to act. For what may be a hard task for the other nations, that is to turn back in the on-rushing stream of life—because they consider themselves united by time and space and only on festive days and in hours of destiny do they feel as members in a chain of generations—this is just the very basis of our communal and individual life: the feeling of being our fathers' children, our grandchildren's ancestors. Therefore we may rightly expect to find ourselves again, at some time, somehow, in our fathers' every word and deed; and also that our own words and deeds will have some meaning for our grandchildren. For we are, as Scripture puts it, "children"; we are, as tradition reads it, "Builders."

I have said what I wanted to say. Did I say it to you? Certainly so, insofar as my words refer to your lecture, and insofar as that lecture induced me to express things I would otherwise have only expressed after a full life's experience. I could not believe that you, who have shown us again the one path to the Torah, should be unable to see what moves us as well today along the other path. I could do no more than show you what we experience. Therefore I may well hope that my words will be accepted by you with an open eye, for they are rather addressed to your eye than to your ear.

Something else weighs heavily upon me. I did not speak for myself alone; that would have been arrogant, and not in accordance with what I had to say. But I cannot tell you the names of the "We" from whose mouths I spoke. Not a few people I know are included, and possibly more whom I do not know. But hardly any of them would agree with everything I said here. Nevertheless I speak for them too. For my words open up a dialogue which I hope will be carried on with deeds and with the conduct of life rather than with words. And I hope that this dialogue shall not come to rest any more among those whom I have included in "We." Then my words which have only opened the dialogue may well die away in theirs. The first word was only spoken for the sake of the last. And this premature "We" shall at one time be silent in the last one.

APPENDICES

UPON OPENING THE JÜDISCHES LEHRHAUS

Draft of an Address

Today, as the Lehrhaus opens its doors to carry on the series of Jewish adult education courses which were attempt to emulate the revered man[1] whose splendid address launched our last winter's activities by taking a subject from the vast field of Jewish scholarship. Nor would you expect it of me, younger and unknown as I am. I intend only to give you an account of the task we have set ourselves and the goals we have in mind, and I shall try to formulate these in the simplest of words.

Learning—there are by now, I should say, very few among you unable to catch the curious note the word sounds, even today, when it is used in a Jewish context. It is to a book, the Book, that we owe our survival— that Book which we use, not by accident, in the very form in which it has existed for millenia: it is the only book of antiquity that is still in living use as a scroll.[2] The learning of this book became an affair of the people, fill-ing the bounds of Jewish life, completely. Everything was really within this learning of the Book. There have been "outside books,"[3] but studying them was looked upon as the first step toward heresy. Occasionally such "outside" elements—Aristotle, for example—have been successfully naturalized. But in the past few centuries the strength to do this would seem to have petered out.

Then came the Emancipation. At one blow it vastly enlarged the intellectual horizons of thought and soon, very soon afterwards, of actual living. Jewish "studying" or "learning" has not been able to keep pace with this rapid extension. What is new is not so much the collapse of the outer barriers; even previously, while the ghetto had certainly sheltered the Jew, it had not shut him off. He moved beyond its bounds, and what the ghetto gave him was only peace, home, a home for his spirit. What is new, is not that the Jew's feet could now take him farther than ever before—in the Middle Ages the Jew was not an especially sedentary, but rather a comparatively mobile element of medieval society. The new feature is that the wanderer no longer returns at dusk. The gates of the ghetto no longer close behind him, allowing him to spend the night in solitary learning. To abandon the figure of speech—he finds his spiritual and intellectual home outside the Jewish world.

The old style of learning is helpless before this spiritual emigration. In vain have both Orthodoxy and Liberalism tried to expand into and fill the new domains. No matter how much Jewish Law was stretched, it lacked the power to encompass and assimilate the life of the intellect and the spirit. The *mezuzah* may have still greeted one at the door, but the bookcase had, at best, a single

Jewish corner. And Liberalism fared no better, even though it availed itself of the nimble air squadron of ideas rather than trying to master life by engaging it in hand-to-hand combat with the Law. There was nothing to be done apparently, except dilute the spirit of Judaism (or what passed for it) as much as possible in order to stake off the whole area of intellectual life; to fill it in the true sense was out of the question. High-sounding words were always on tap, words that the Judaism of old had had, but which it was chary of uttering for fear of dulling their edges with too frequent use. High sounding words, like "humanity," "idealism," and so forth, which those who mouthed them thought as encompassing the whole world. But the world resists such superficial embraces. It is impossible to assimilate to Judaism a field of intellectual and spiritual life through constantly reiterating a catchword and then claiming it to have kinship with some Jewish concept or other. The problems of democracy, for instance, cannot be Judaized merely by referring to the sentence in the Torah: "One law and one ordinance shall be both for you and for the stranger that sojourneth with you" (Numbers 15:16), nor those of socialism by citing certain social institutions or social programs in ancient Israel. If we insist on trying, so much the worse for us! For the great, the creative spirits in our midst, have never allowed themselves to be deceived. They have left us. They went everywhere, they found their own spiritual homes, and they created spiritual homes for others. The Book around which we once gathered stands forlorn in this world, and even for those who regard it as a beloved duty to return to it at regular intervals, such a return is nothing but a turning away from life, a turning one's back on life. Their world remains un-Jewish even when they still have a Jewish world to return to. "Learning"—the old form of maintaining the relationship between life and the Book—has failed.

Has it really? No, only in the old form. For down at heel as we are, we should not be a sign and a wonder among the peoples, we should not be the eternal people, if our very illness did not beget its own cure. It is now as it has always been. We draw new strength from the very circumstance that seemed to deal the death blow to "learning," from the desertion of our scholars to the realms of the alien knowledge of the "outside books," from the transformation of our erstwhile *talmide hakhamim*[4] into the instructors and professors of modern European universities. A new "learning" is about to be born— rather, it has been born.

It is a learning in reverse order. A learning that no longer starts from the Torah and leads into life, but the other way round: from life, from a world that knows nothing of the Law, or pretends to know nothing, back to the Torah. That is the sign of the time.

It is the sign of the time because it is the mark of the men of the time. There is no one today who is not alienated, or who does not contain within himself some small fraction of alienation. All of us to whom Judaism, to whom being a Jew, has again become the pivot of our lives—and I know that in saying this here I am not speaking for myself alone—we all know that in being Jews we must not give up anything, not renounce anything, but lead everything back to Judaism. From the periphery back to the center; from the outside, in.

This is a new sort of learning. A learning for which—
in these days—he is the most apt who brings with him the
maximum of what is alien. That is to say, *not* the man
specializing in Jewish matters; or, if he happens to be
such a specialist, he will succeed, not in the capacity of
a specialist, but only as one who, too, is alienated, as one
who is groping his way home.

It is not a matter of pointing out relations between
what is Jewish and what is non-Jewish. There has been
enough of that. It is not a matter of apologetics, but
rather of finding the way back into the heart of our life.
And of being confident that this heart is a Jewish heart.
For we are Jews.

That sounds very simple. And so it is. It is really
enough to gather together people of all sorts as teachers
and students. Just glance at our prospectus. You will find,
listed among others, a chemist, a physician, a historian,
an artist, a politician. Two-thirds of the teachers are persons who, twenty or thirty years ago, in the only century
when Jewish learning had become the monopoly of spe-
cialists, would have been denied the right of teaching in
a Jewish House of Study. They have come together here
as Jews. They have come together in order to "learn"—
for Jewish "learning" includes Jewish "teaching." Whoever teaches here—and I believe I may say this in the
name of all who are teaching here—knows that in teaching here he need sacrifice nothing of what he is. Whoever
gathers—and all of us are "gatherers"—must seize upon
that which is to be gathered wherever he finds it. And
more than this: he must seize upon himself as well, wherever he may find himself. Were we to do otherwise, we
should continue in the errors of a century and perpetuate

the failure of that century: the most we could do would
be to adorn life with a few "pearls of thought" from the
Talmud or some other source, and—for the rest—leave
it just as un-Jewish as we found it. But no: we take life
as we find it. Our own life and the life of our students;
and gradually (or, at times, suddenly) we carry this life
from the periphery where we found it to the center. And
we ourselves are carried only by a faith which certainly
cannot be proved, the faith that this center can be nothing
but a Jewish center.

This faith must remain without proof. It carries further
than our word. For we hail from the periphery. The oneness of the center is not something that we possess clearly
and unambiguously, not something we can be articulate
about. Our fathers were better off in that respect. We are
not so well off today. We must search for this oneness
and have faith that we shall find it. Seen from the periphery, the center does not appear invariably the same. In
fact, the center of the circle looks different from each
point of the periphery. There are many ways that lead
from the outside in. Nevertheless, the inside is oneness
and harmony. In the final analysis, everyone here should
be speaking about the same thing. And he who speaks as
he should, will in the end really have spoken about exactly
what everyone else has spoken about. Only the outset,
only the point of departure, will be different for everyone.

So, and only so, will you be able to understand the
divisions and contrasts in our prospectus.[5] The contrasts
are put in solely for the purpose of being bridged. Today
what is classical, historical, and modern in Judaism may
be placed side by side, but this ought not to be so and in
the future will not be so. It is up to us to discover the

root-fibres of history in the classical phase, and its harvest in the modern. Whatever is genuinely Jewish must be all three simultaneously. Such has been the case in Judaism in all its productive periods. And we shall leave it to those who stand on the outside to consider contrasts such as that between the Torah and the Prophets, between Halakhah and Haggadah, between world and man, as real contrasts which cannot be reconciled. So far as we are concerned, which one of us is not certain that there could be no Torah without the prophetic powers of Moses, father of all prophets before him and after him? And—on the other hand—that there could be no prophets without the foundation of a Law and an order from which their prophecy derived its rule and measure? As for any contrast between Halakhah and Haggadah—every page of the Talmud shows the student that the two are inseparably intertwined, and every page of Jewish history confirms that the same minds and hearts are preoccupied with both: scholarly inquiry and meditation, legal decision *and* scriptural exegesis. And, finally, the Jewish world! Who could imagine that it would be possible to build it up without man, Jewish man! And what—in the long run—will become of Jewish man if, no matter where he lives, he is not surrounded by an atmosphere Jewish to some degree, by a Jewish world?

So, all of this hangs together. More than that: it is one and the same within itself, and as such it will be presented to you here. You should regard every individual aspect, every individual lecture or seminar you attend, as a part of the whole, which is offered to you only for the sake of the whole.

It is in this sense that now, at the opening of the new

term in this hall, I bid you welcome. May the hours you
spend here become hours of remembrance, but not in the
stale sense of a dead piety that is so frequently the attitude toward Jewish matters. I mean hours of another kind
of remembrance, an inner remembering, a turning from
externals to that which is within, a turning that, believe
me, will and must become for you a returning home.
Turn into yourself, return home to your innermost self
and to your innermost life.

MORE JUDAISM!

Two Letters

Franz Rosenzweig to Richard Ehrenberg

December 28, 1917

Dear Uncle:

I thank you for your kind letter. To the point: The general schedule of instruction, adopted by the Rabbinical assembly in 1916, puts historical considerations—in a very clever way, from the general and from the Jewish point of view—to the center. (The minutes of the assembly, printed by a Frankfort publishing house, are quite interesting). In my *Zeit ists* (*It Is Time*) I have consciously moved the sources to the center and history to the periphery. The reason: History—you will believe me that I do not underestimate this field—is, if it were the *main* weapon, a *double*-edged sword; he who has no other relation to Judaism can be led astray by history as well, if more easily, than being strengthened by it . . . It is quite different for him who has already some access to Judaism; for him it can certainly be a weapon—a shield, however, not a sword. The "sword" may be Jewish ethnic consciousness (as the Zionists know better than I do, although I do not deny it altogether) or Jewish life (where this exists I have nothing to add). And yet what is still missing, what is so much out of order in our lives? It is: Jewish *spirit*. The school can not do much, but if it can do anything at all, it is this: transmit the spirit. In this respect, we are in as fortunate a situation as the general school, if it wants to transmit the German spirit: it only has to inspire, to introduce, to arouse respect; the rest, and the essential, is supplied by the grand lessons from life—the theatre, the subscription,—and chamber music concerts. Our lesson from life lies in the synagogue. The school has only to—see above. The more intensively, the more one-sidedly the instruction has this aim, namely the synagogue, the less it will lead to conflicts at home. It will ignore the home to a certain degree. This is not an ideal. It is even a slap in the face of the Jewish ideal ("makes void the teaching"), but, at a time where it is important to work for the Lord, one *may* "make the teaching void," as the Talmud once explains the Psalm verse in a famous passage, and I had this explanation too in mind, when I wrote this verse above and below my pamphlet.

You see, all these things are interrelated.

The main thing is that anything is being done at all, "to work" (as the Psalm has it) (and about the same way it is in the army regulations, only with slightly different words: "to do nothing at all is worse than an error in the choice of the means").

Best regards to you and dear Aunt.

Yours, F.

Franz Rosenzweig to Hedwig Cohn-Vohssen

March 7, 1918

Dear Madam:

It is true that the point of view is 'quite different, but we are certainly not "very far apart"; maybe you are removed from me, but I am not far removed from you.

In the first instance, to settle this right away: I knew of your Zionist convictions; Hermann Badt[1] had told me about them. If I turned to you in spite of this, it is because I believe that Jewish theology is something which concerns all Jews without consideration of their leanings. Goethe once said in a rather Mephistophelian mood to his disciple Eckermann: "I have always found that it is good to know something;" and similarly I think that everybody would benefit by a Science of Judaism made more accessible than before. To me personally parties do not matter; I wish both of them, the Zionists and the members of the Central-Verein,[2] to become a little more—Jewish. It is for this reason that I really wrote the pamphlet [*It Is Time*]. All it was supposed to do was to arouse them a bit. The movement for the creation of the "Academy" should not refer to it; it should cease and be forgotten after having done its work. If it were a program and not a fanfare, it would hardly have been possible that Heinrich Loewe [the Zionist] was among the first ones to sign the appeal for the creation of the Academy. So you see I do not yet consider your refusal to be final; I still hope. Your Stephan may not need it any more. But Stephan has many, many brethren who do need it and whom you—to use Max Brod's beautiful poem[3] in the Jewish Almanac—"did not love enough,"

if you leave them only the road to Zionism, and if you
do not accept them, even if it be only for the time being,
the way they are. Perhaps if you now meet them on their
own ground, they may be better prepared to join you.
Perhaps. Anyhow—the kick which sends the brother into
nothingness just because he does not want what I want—
this is sectarians' policy. Therefore something quite un-
Jewish. For even if one feels one belongs to the "remnant," this feeling should not become the principle for
one's actions (only a source of strength). The principle
for action remains: *Klal Yisrael* [the community of
Israel as a whole].

I have now reached the main content of your letter.
May I say which phrase has haunted me continuously
since I read your letter? At the outset you will perhaps
laugh. The phrase is "petty Jewish" (*kleinjüdisch*). As
there are petty Germans, petty Englishmen, so the Zionists of your type (I know that they are not dominant any
more, certainly not by themselves) are petty Jews. And
only then did I realize that my point of view should
really be called all-Jewish. True, I do not write the word
"humanity" with quotation marks, as you do: but rather
for the most part I do not use this word at all or, if I
do write it, I write it without such fig leaves of the spirit.
If I were to write "humanity," I ought also to write Jewish "people." But I do write Jewish people. Only the
"publicly and legally assured national home" can do
without quotation marks. And just because of that, because I had always, even *before* the war, considered it a
goal to be attained easily and soon, I was never much
interested in it. Why not this road too! there are so many
roads. But I cannot see *the* road in it. Therefore I must

include Zionism in my Jewish sentiment, although it excludes me from its own. This is what I meant before: I am closer to you than you are to me. It appears to me as if my feeling concerning the Zionist narrowing down of Judaism were similar to your feeling towards orthodoxy. So terribly benevolent. Moreover, it is hardly necessary to protect orthodoxy so anxiously from the draft of science. It does that anyhow, as far as necessary; it winds a thick scarf around its neck, but then exposes itself quite unconcernedly to the draft. And the arrogance would impress me more if it were turned more against the outside and not mainly against everything un-orthodox within Judaism. I have had some astounding experience in this respect. But this is not important. Orthodoxy and Zionism are certainly conserving powers, Zionism even more than merely conserving, since it returns to us even those who had already been far removed. If it had taken hold of the majority of German Jews, I might have addressed *It Is Time* to Martin Buber. Because more Buber is as necessary for the Zionists as more Cohen is necessary for the members of the Central-Verein. More Judaism. (I should, however, add that Cohen is originally much more Jewish. At first I had thought that the ideas of the two complement one another like two hemispheres. But recently I have found that Cohen's ideas are already a globe by themselves). Anyhow, I was concerned with the majority, and this is—Rathenau.[4] One *cannot* drop these people, they are too valuable, and even if they were not—but then again they are. And I do not agree with you that everything has been done what could have been done for the Rathenaus. "Jewish scholars in Berlin," this is just not enough; there are too many things "in

Berlin." But there must be a Jewish theological department within the German *universitas literarum* (and of
course within all others too)—then the Rathenaus cannot
disregard it any more. Walter Rathenau has *not* overcome
Judaism as a religion, he only thinks he has. To make
this impossible or at least extremely hard, is not the task
of individual scholars, but only the visible existence of
an "ism." At present the Rathenaus are as naive as children; *then* they will at least know what they are doing.
And fifty per cent of the time they will do it anyhow.
But fifty other per cent they will not, and my hope is in
these. There is doubtless an element of smuggling in this:
I would like to bring in Judaism through the backdoor
of "general education," the kind of education the Rathenaus want so much. The German Jew will have to be
ashamed of knowing as little as most of them do now.
Some beginnings of these feelings of shame can already
be seen, at least in some of the younger people. Buber's
monthly *Der Jude* has a big part in this, I think. He
too is smuggling. The cover address is: To the Intellec-
tuals. But inside speaks Rabbi Martin Solomonides.[5]

I had more on my mind, but this letter does not seem
to acquire a shape anyhow. I am writing under terrible
conditions, on the knee—this takes the blame for my
handwriting and the lack of cohesion of this letter. And,
alas! the furlough is still in my bones; I am not set for
war yet—if I am ever.

Thank you anyhow for your nice letter, and do not
take offense with this ugly one from

Yours,

FRANZ ROSENZWEIG.

REVELATION AND LAW

Martin Buber and Franz Rosenzweig

Martin Buber to Franz Rosenzweig

Heppenheim, September 28, 1922

Dear Dr. Rosenzweig:

How could you assume that I treat you with "expressive silence"—a means of communication which, incidentally, I am neither willing nor able to employ—? I am sure you realized, after the first half hour of your visit to my home at Heppenheim that I talked to you in a way I wished I could talk to all human beings—a Messianic wish indeed: in that world people take things in good grace, and if they refrain from talking, they do so either because they *wish* to be silent or because they *cannot* talk. The reason for my not answering your letter of last Friday is that, at this stage of our talk, I might have been able to go on talking, but I was unable to write. The problem coud no longer be discussed objectively; the question had become a personal one, and, referring to your example of the Pantheon,[1] I would have had to tell

you about the internal and even external history of my
own youth, for instance, how once on a Day of Atonement I caused annoyance (in a liberal synagogue) by
following the tradition of bending my knee and prostrat-
ing myself while reciting the words, "We bend our knee
and prostrate ourselves" . . .

Martin Buber to Franz Rosenzweig

Heppenheim, October 1, 1922
(Eve of the Day of Atonement)

But I must still tell you something serious: that in
spite of everything, I feel in my innermost heart that
today is the Eve of Yom Kippur. This may be so because
(if I may add an autobiographical note) between my
thirteenth and fourteenth year (when I was fourteen I
stopped putting on my Tefillin) I experienced this day
with a force unequalled by any other experience since.
And do you think that I was a "child" at that time?
Maybe less so than now, and this in a poignant sense;
at that time I took Space and Time seriously; I did not
hold back as I do now. And then, when the sleepless night
was heavy upon me and very real, my body, already
reacting to the fast, became as important to me as an
animal marked for sacrifice. This is what formed me:
the night, and the following morning, and the Day itself,
with all its hours, not omitting a single moment. So you
see I had not originally been exposed to "liberal" influ-
ences in my religious education.

The annoyance mentioned previously occurred in the
Temple (sic!) in Lemberg, where I went only when my
father wished to lure me away from my grandfather who
liked to take me to a small hasidic *Klaus*. He, an "en-
lightened" Jew, a Maskil, liked to pray among the Has-

idim and used a prayer book full of mystical directions.

All this is not only past but present, and yet I am the way I am: with much imperfection, yet nothing is felt to be missing any more. May your good heart understand me!

May you be sealed for a good life.

Yours,

MARTIN BUBER.

Martin Buber to Franz Rosenzweig

Heppenheim, June 24, 1924

Dear Friend:

I hear that at first you had agreed to have *The Builders* published but then had reconsidered. I would like to recommend to you that you have it printed, no matter how it had originally been announced. I would prefer to have that epistle published by itself. If I am able to write an answer, it will contain nothing in disagreement with its details. I agree to everything that follows from the letter's premises, but not to those premises themselves. It is my faith that prevents me from doing this. You know, my dear, that I do not use this word lightly, and yet here it is quite appropriate. I do not believe that *revelation* is ever a formulation of law. It is only through man in his self-contradiction that revelation becomes legislation. This is the fact of man. I cannot admit the law transformed by man into the realm of my will, if I am to hold myself ready as well for the unmediated word of God directed to a specific hour of life.

It is part of my being that I cannot accept both [the

Law and the word of God] together and I cannot imagine
that this position will ever change for me. Other people
may have a different attitude. This, though appearing in-
comprehensible to me, nevertheless I respect. But I cannot approach the fact of the Law, nor even its concept
except from the point of view of my faith. As a matter
of fact, it was during the past week that I have most
urgently experienced (an experience that even penetrated
my dreams) that this is impossible, even "scientifically"
impossible.

Should my reply to your letter contain therefore all
this and other disquieting matters related to it upon which
I have not touched here? I cannot count on the present-
day reader—the public being so deplorably casual as to
vouchsafe without obligation anything and everything they
read or hear. In a reply I would have to stake my very
being. Such a personal commitment, though perhaps in
store for me later, would require a more thorough bath
of purification than I am capable of at this moment.

Cordially yours,

MARTIN BUBER.

Franz Rosenzweig to Martin Buber

June 29, 1924

Dear Friend:

Please bring along *The Builders* this coming Wednes-
day, so that I shall be able to read it again, since I do
not remember the details too well.

In your recent letter there was a sentence which has
frightened me again and again: it is the one in which

you state that between yourself and "other people" there is a partition which makes their position inconceivable, although you respect it. This seems untenable. Such a respect has its place in life which always means separation; but in the realm of faith it is impossible, since faith must always be able to bind together, all separations and everything hard to understand is so only temporarily and cannot call for lasting respect. I deeply respect your different way of life; but you must not respect my different faith; that would stand in the way of the ultimate goal, which must be: the union of all minds in spite of the existent difference in the way of life.

And, besides—do we really differ in faith? Even for him who observes the Law, revelation is not what you call law-giving. "On this day"[2]—that is his theory of experience as well as yours. He as well as you deems it unfortunate that the commandment issued "on that day" should give rise to the old law. We do not consciously accept the fact that every commandment can become law, but that the law can always be changed back into a commandment, a fact which you know so well . . . As far as faith is concerned, the difference between us is a small one, nothing inconceivable.

Martin Buber to Franz Rosenzweig

Heppenheim, July 1, 1924

Dear Friend:

I welcome what you say about "respect." What I meant was: to "respect" something we cannot yet comprehend. I am willing, however, to change "respect" to "accept." However, as I said, I cannot comprehend it yet (as, in the sphere of greater vastness and awe, I cannot comprehend the belief in God's own son, with due consideration for the difference!)

But this matter itself is more difficult than you think: for, you fail to consider, I believe, that it is the fact of man that brings about transformation from revelation to what you call commandment [*Gebot*]. Permit me to express this so dryly, without adding anything . . .

Martin Buber to Franz Rosenzweig

Heppenheim, July 5, 1924

Dear Friend:

Of course I misunderstood you, of course I cannot draw a dividing line between revelation and the command to Abraham "Get thee out" (Genesis 12:1); nor between revelation and "I am the Lord thy God" (Exodus 20:2); but I must draw it between revelation and "Thou shalt have no other gods" (Verse 3). I do know that he who explained his position with the words, "I stood between the Lord and you" (Deuteronomy 5:5) could, after having said, "I am the Lord thy God," continue only with, "Thou shalt have no other gods." But the fact that they and I had to be told this, and justifyingly told, from this idea I have to be redeemed. It is this fact which explains why I cannot accept the laws and the statutes blindly, but I must ask myself again and again: Is this particular law addressed to me and rightly so? So that at one time I may include myself in this Israel which is addressed, but at times, many times, I cannot. And if there is anything that I can call without reservation a *Mitzvah* within my own sphere, it is just this that I act as I do.

I cannot go on with this communication, incomplete

though it is. Your good heart will complete it so that it
will yield an adequate meaning.

Cordially yours,

MARTIN BUBER.

Martin Buber to Franz Rosenzweig

Heppenheim, July 13, 1924.

Dear Friend:

No, it is not clear to me. I told you that for me, though
man is a law-receiver, God is not a law-giver, and therefore the Law has no universal validity for me, but only
a personal one. I accept, therefore, only what I think is
being spoken to me (e.g., the older I become, and the
more I realize the restlessness of my soul, the more I
accept for myself the Day of Rest). *The Builders* want
to make me accept the Law as something universal, the
way I accept Teaching as something to be learned in its
totality. The analogy you suggest does not exist. You will
realize indirectly that this is so when you consider that
we can atone for what we have done, but not for what
one has experienced. This indicates that the deed differs
not only quantitatively from experience, but qualitatively.
You will realize this *directly* as well when you consider
how different the two are in relation to the fact which
concerns us here, the fact of the imperative, not the philosophical, but the divine and the human one, for I am
responsible for what I do or leave undone in a different
way than for what I learn or leave unlearned. Therefore
the division between revelation and teaching (human
teaching) is for me neither a thorn nor a trial, but that
between revelation and law (human law) is both . . .

Franz Rosenzweig to Martin Buber

July 16, 1924

It is true that there is no analogy between learning and doing, but there is an analogy between thinking and doing. You can really "repent" for your thoughts. The great turn in my own life occurred in the realms of thoughts, although deeds depended on the thoughts too. What so far had been permitted or even commanded was not allowed any more. But this was only the consequence. And looking back later, I was not so much frightened by the deeds, which, after all, had only been consequences, but by the whole world of ideas in which I had lived, a kind of Barthianism,[3] as I must have told you.

That the separation of revelation and teaching is for you also a thorn and a trial, this you will readily admit when in speaking of teaching you do not think of petty Midrashim, but of the Christian dogma. Yes, we are responsible, not for what we learn or fail to learn, but for what we think or fail to think.

For me, too, God is not a Law-giver. But He commands. It is only by the manner of his observance that man in his inertia changes the commandments into Law, a legal system with paragraphs, without the realization that "I am the Lord,"[4] without "fear and trembling,"[5] without the awareness that the man stands under God's commandment. Could this, then, be the difference between us? Possibly, but not necessarily. If, e.g., F.Ch. Rang's political views would change from a matter of conscience to a petty organization, I would accept that as a confirmation of the rule that a commandment changes into a law and I would say with the Greeks: "It is not God's fault."

But if the "On this day" becomes a Shulhan Arukh[6] then I turn a bit pantheistic and believe that it does concern God. Because He has sold Himself to us with his Torah. But in the end we share even this faith.

I hope that in London[7] you will not only enjoy success in our cause, but also the beautiful city itself. Both of us envy you.

Cordially yours,

FRANZ ROSENZWEIG.

Martin Buber to Franz Rosenzweig

Heppenheim, June 3, 1925

Dear Friend:

For me the one question which is sounded in my soul from abyss to abyss is: Is the Law God's Law? The other answer to this question is not mere silence. If, however, the answer were "Yes," I would not meditate on whether the Law is a force making for the wholeness of life, for such would then be immaterial. On the other hand, no other "Yes" can replace the missing affirmation. This missing "Yes" is not quietly absent: its absence is noted with terror.

Franz Rosenzweig to Martin Buber

June 5, 1925

Dear Friend:

The question concerning the Law, as well as the one concerning God Himself, should not be treated in the "third person." I, too, do not know whether the Law "is" God's law. I know that as little, and even less than I know that God "is." Knowledge or ignorance is not valid when an experience has been made. As far as you have made the experience that the Law is not God's law—and it is this experience on which your sentence is based—that is a valid one, as valid as an atheism based on an experience that God does not exist: whereas he who does not know that God exists, or whether God exists, must not frighten us.

Thus revelation is certainly not Law-giving. It is only this: Revelation. The primary content of revelation is revelation itself. "He came down" [on Sinai]—this already concludes the revelation; "He spoke" is the beginning of interpretation, and certainly "I am." But where does this "interpretation" stop being legitimate? I would never dare to state this in a general sentence; here commences the right of experience to give testimony, positive and negative.

Or could it be that revelation must never become legislation? Because then the original self-interpretation of revelation would have to give way to human interpretation? This I would admit, just as I am convinced that revelation cannot be identified with a human person. But, in spite of this my conviction, as I concede to a Christian a historic and personal right to prove an exception, so I believe in the right of the Law to prove its character as an exception against all other types of law. This is the point where the question put forward in *The Builders* claims to be an answer to your question. A question thus becomes an answer to a question! This may not satisfy the first inquirer, but it makes it difficult for him to give an answer based on his life "today" because it opens up for him a view of tomorrow. This must be your position as regards *The Builders*.

THE COMMANDMENTS:

Divine or Human?

A Letter[1]

I was startled by Nahum Glatzer's words that only the election of the people of Israel has divine origin, but all the details of the Law came from man alone. I should have formulated this—and have actually done so to myself—in very much the same way, but when one hears one's own ideas uttered by someone else, they suddenly become problematic. Can we really draw so rigid a boundary between what is divine and what is human? We must keep in mind the obvious fact that a Law as a whole, is the prerequisite for being chosen, the law whereby divine election is turned into human electing, and the passive state of a people being chosen and set apart is changed into the activity on the people's side of doing the deed which sets it apart. The only matter of doubt is whether or to what degree this Law originating in Israel's election coincides with the traditional Jewish law. But here our doubt must be genuine doubt, which willingly listens to reason and is as willing to be swayed to a "yes" as to a "no."

In my thinking about this, another differentiation occurred to me: the differentiation between what can be *stated* about God and what can be *experienced* about God. What can be stated objectively is only the very general formula "God exists." Experience, however, goes much further. What we can thus state—or even prove—about God is related to our possible "experience" in the same way that the empty announcement that two persons have married, or the showing of the marriage certificate, is related to the daily and hourly reality of this marriage. The reality cannot be communicated to a third person; it is no one's concern and yet it is the only thing that counts, and the objective statement of the fact of marriage would be meaningless without this most private, incommunicable reality. And so even the bare fact of marriage does not become real save where it leaves the sphere of what can be objectively stated and enters the secret pale of the festive days and anniversaries of private life.

It is exactly the same with what man experiences about God: it is incommunicable, and he who speaks of it makes himself ridiculous. Modesty must veil this aloneness-together. Yet everyone knows that though unutterable it is not a self-delusion (which a third person might well think it! It is your own fault if you run within striking distance of the psychologist's knife! Why did you blab?). Here, too, it is man's own experience—utterly inexpressible—that is the fulfillment and realization of utterable truth. All that is needed is—to undergo this experience.

And now I suggest that the matter of the details of the Law is analogous to the wealth of experiences, of which only that experience holds which is in the act of being undergone, and holds only for him who is undergoing it. Here too there is no rigid boundary in the relationship between God and man. Here too the only boundary lies between what can and what cannot be expressed. What can be expressed, what can be formulated in terms of theology, so that a Christian too could understand it as an "article of faith," is the connection between election and the Law. But an outsider, no matter how willing and sympathetic, can never be made to accept a single commandment as a "religious" demand. We wholly realize that general theological connection only when we cause it to come alive by fulfilling individual commandments, and transpose it from the objectivity of a theological truth to the "Thou" of the benediction: when he who is called to the reading of the Torah unites, in his benediction before and after the reading, thanks for the "national" election from among the peoples of the earth with thanks for the "religious" election to eternal life.

Here too the incomprehensibility from the viewpoint of religion, of the individual commandment does not constitute incomprehensibility per se. Just as a student of William James knows how to put every "religious experience" into the correct cubbyhole of the psychology of religion, and a Freudian student can analyze the experience into its elements of the old yet ever new story, so a student of Wellhausen[2] will trace every commandment back to its human, folkloristic origin, and a student of Max Weber[3] derive it from the special structure of a people. Psychological analysis finds the solution to all enigmas in self-delusion, and historical sociology finds it in mass delusion. The Law is not understood as a commandment addressed by God to the people but as a soliloquy of the people. We know it differently, not always and not in all things, but again and again. For we know it only when—we *do*.

What do we know when we do? Certainly not that all of these historical and sociological explanations are false. But in the light of the doing, of the right doing in which we experience the reality of the Law, the explanations are of superficial and subsidiary importance. And, in the doing there is even less room for the converse wisdom (which in hours of weakness and emptiness we gladly clutch at for comfort), that these historical and sociological explanations may be true, and that Law is important because it alone guarantees the unity of the people in space and through time. Such timid insight lies behind and beneath the moment of doing in which we experience just this moment; it is this experience of the theo-human reality of the commandment that permits us to pray: "Blessed art Thou . . ."

In this immediacy we may not "express" God [*Gott aussprechen*], but rather address God [*Gott ansprechen*] in the individual commandment. For whoever seeks to express him will discover that he who cannot be expressed will become he who cannot be found. Only in the commandment can the voice of him who commands be heard. No matter how well the written word may fit in with our own thoughts, it cannot give us the faith that creation is completed, to the degree that we experience this by keeping the Sabbath, and inaugurating it with, "And the heaven and the earth were completed." Not that doing necessarily results in hearing and understanding. But one hears differently when one hears in the doing. All the days of the year Balaam's talking ass may be a mere fairy tale, but not on the Sabbath wherein this portion is read in the synagogue, when it speaks to me out of the open Torah. But if not a fairy tale, what then? I cannot say right now; if I should think about it today, when it is past, and try to say what it is, I should probably only utter the platitude that it is a fairy tale. But on that day, in that very hour, it is—well, certainly not a fairy tale, but that which is communicated to me provided I am able to fulfill the command of the hour, namely, to open my ears.

What can be expressed marks the beginning of our way. This is peculiar to our situation, which we must not ignore but see as clearly as possible. The situation of the Jew who never left the fold is different. Jacob Rosenheim[4] once told a young man who confessed to him that he believed in nothing but loved every single commandment: "You need have no misgivings in keeping them all. But, for the time being, do not let yourself be called to the reading of the Torah." So far as we are concerned, just this *mitzvah* which leads from what can to what cannot be expressed is nearest our hearts, while many of the others are alien to us. Our way has led back to the whole, but we are still seeking the individual parts.

Thus, I do not think the boundary between the divine and the human is that between the whole and the parts, but that between something whose origin we recognize with a recognition which can be expressed, communicated, and formulated, and something else whose origin we also recognize and recognize just as clearly, but with a recognition which cannot be expressed and communicated. I should not venture to dub "human" any commandment whatsoever, just because it has not yet been vouchsafed me to say over it: "Blessed art *Thou*." Nor can I imagine the divine nature of the whole (which I, like you, believe in) in any other sense than of Rabbi Nobel's powerful five-minute sermon on God's appearing before Abraham's tent: "And *God* appeared to Abraham . . . and he lifted his eyes . . . and behold: three *men*."

Greeting to all four of you from your old friend who is very happy to see the signs of fresh life in the Lehrhaus.

FRANZ ROSENZWEIG.

NOTES

It Is Time: *Concerning the Study of Judaism*

[*Zeit ists. Kleinere Schriften*, pp. 56-78]

1   According to the German school system valid at the time of the conception of this essay, all children spent the first four years in the Basic School (*Grundschule*). Then they either entered the People's School (*Volksschule*), which offered a general curriculum of four years, or a High School, which led to graduation at the age of fifteen or, for those who wanted to go to college, at the age of eighteen. There were two types of high schools: those concentrating on science and modern languages, and those emphasizing classical languages. In either case the teaching of the first of the two obligatory languages was commenced at the age of ten, i.e., first year of high school. (Translator's note.)

2   *Amidah*: Central prayer recited standing in silent devotion.

3   *Maoz Tzur*: A popular Hanukkah song.

4   "Our Father, our King," a prayer for the Days of Repentence.

5   Talmudic tractate dealing with ethics and the study of the Torah.

6   In Germany, as in other European countries, schools were in session on Saturdays.

7   In German schools, each period consisted of 45 minutes of instruction and 15 minutes of recess.

8   See note 1.

9   Philo (1st cent.), Jewish-Hellenist philosopher in Alexandria.

10   Saadia (10th cent.), religious philosopher in Babylonia.

11   Solomon Ibn Gabirol (11th cent.), Hebrew poet and philosopher in Spain.

12   Abraham Ibn Ezra (12th cent.), poet and Bible commentator in Spain.

13   Judah ha-Levi (11th-12th cent.), classical Hebrew poet.

14   Moses Maimonides (12th cent.), classical Jewish philosopher.

15   Levi ben Gershon (14th cent.), religious philosopher.

16   Joseph Albo (14th-15th cent.), religious philosopher in Spain.

17   Joseph Karo (16th cent.), author of a code of Jewish law (*Shulhan Arukh*).

18   Moses Isserles (16th cent.), wrote glosses to the *Shulhan Arukh.*

19   Leopold Zunz (19th cent.), founder of the "Science of Judaism."

20   Presentation of Judaism by Judah ha-Levi.

21   "Dogmas," by Joseph Albo.

22   Principal philosophical work by Maimonides.

23   System of Jewish ethics, by Bahya Ibn Pakuda, 11th cent.

24   Foremost work of Jewish mysticism; 13th cent.

25   Isaac Luria (16th cent.), leader of Safed Kabbalistic movement.

26   In high schools in Germany, only minor subjects were taught in the afternoon periods.

27   Leopold Zunz.

28   Halakhah: Jewish law.

29   Aggadah, or Haggadah: Extra-legal, ethical, theological, poetic parts of Jewish teachings.

30   This would be equivalent to about $2,500 under present living conditions.

Towards a Rennaissance of Jewish Learning

[*Bildung und kein Ende. Kleinere Schriften*, pp. 79-93]

1   Max Brod (b. 1884), novelist, Jewish thinker and editor of Kafka's works.

2   Torah combined with "general culture"; educational principle of neo-orthodoxy in Germany.

The Builders: Concerning the Law

[*Die Bauleute. Kleinere Schriften*, pp. 107-113]

[1]   Buber, *Reden über des Judentum*, ("Lectures on Judaism"), Frankfort 1923.

[2]   *Herut*: a lecture on youth and religion.

[3]   A heathen asked Hillel (1st cent.) to explain to him the entire Torah while he was standing on one foot. Hillel answered: "Do not unto your neighbor what you would not have him do unto you; this is the whole Torah; the rest is commentary; go and learn."

[4]   Originally pertaining to Apocrypha, which were not to be read by a Jew.

[5]   Talmudic master; 2nd cent.

[6]   A heretic; contemporary of Rabbi Akiba.

[7]   Founder of hasidism; 18th cent.

[8]   Samson Raphael Hirsch (1808-1888), founder of neo-orthodoxy in Germany.

[9]   Here and in the following passages, Rosensweig refers to concepts of Jewish tradition as contained in the Talmud and the Midrash.

[10]   A concept of medieval Jewish philosophers.

[11]   Abraham Geiger (1810-1874), leader of Jewish religious liberalism in Germany.

[12]   "Permissible" is here used by Rosensweig to cover that which is excluded from the sphere molded by the Jewish law.

[13]   Proverbs 31:10-31.

[14]   Talmud, Shabbat 88a.

Upon Opening the Jüdisches Lehrhaus

[*Kleinere Schriften*, pp. 94-99]

[1]   Nehemiah A. Nobel (1871-1922), leading rabbi in Frankfort.

[2]   The Torah scrolls that are read in synagogues are written in long-hand on parchment scrolls.

[3]   Apocrypha, "books outside the biblical canon." Here applied to all literature.

[4]   "Disciples of the wise"; religious scholars.

[5]   The courses were divided into three parts: classical, historical, and modern Judaism.

More Judaism

[*Briefe*, pp. 275-276; 283-286]

1   Hermann Badt (1887-1945), high government official; friend of Rosenzweig.
2   A liberal, non-Zionist organization of German Jews mainly for the protection of Jewish rights.
3   "To the Baptized Jews."
4   Assimilated German-Jewish family of industrialists. Walter Rathenau (1867-1922) was a German foreign minister.
5   This refers to Martin Buber's grandfather, Solomon Buber, a noted Hebrew scholar.

Revelation and Law

1   Rosenzweig had used the Pantheon to explain the difference between the outer and the inner aspect of the Law (i.e., whether it is only studied, or also put into practice).
2   Exodus 19:1 with reference to Israel's arrival at Mount Sinai. The classical commentators take "this day" to mean: "The words of the Torah shall always be new to you as if the Torah were given—today."
3   This refers to the theology of Karl Barth.
4   A common conclusion of commandments in the biblical text.
5   In the mystical tradition a Jew is bidden to fulfill a commandment "with fear and trembling."
6   Code of Jewish Law.
7   Buber went to London to negotiate a plan for University and higher popular education in Palestine.

The Commandments: Divine or Human?

[*Briefe*, pp. 518-521]

1   In this letter (November 1924) Rosenzweig reacts to a report on discussions of Judaism at the Freies Jüdisches Lehrhaus. The letter was addressed to the "speakers in the Lehrhaus," Martin Goldner, Nahum Glatzer, Hans Epstein and Lotte Fürth.
2   Julius Wellhausen (1844-1918), German Protestant theologian and Bible critic; he demonstrated an evolution within the original sources of the biblical writings.
3   Max Weber (1864-1920), German sociologist; founder of the so-called "sociology of religion."
4   Jacob Rosenheim (b. 1871), leader of separatist orthodox Judaism (Agudath Yisrael).